and the

AMERICAN REVOLUTION

and the

AMERICAN REVOLUTION

Reverend Alexander Craighead, the Mecklenburg Declaration & the Foothills Fight for Independence

RICHARD P. PLUMER

Published by The History Press
Charleston, SC 29403
www.historypress.net

Front cover: The Hezekiah Alexander House, the oldest in Charlotte. Hezekiah Alexander was a signer of the Mecklenburg Declaration of Independence and an elder in Reverend Alexander Craighead's Hopewell Presbyterian Church. *Courtesy of the Robinson-Spangler Carolina Room, Charlotte Mecklenburg Library*; Portion of the Bishop of London certificate. Mecklenburg's Scotch-Irish Presbyterians were angry that the North Carolina Marriage Act required them to be married by an Anglican minister who had a Bishop of London Certificate, rather than by Reverend Alexander Craighead, their own Presbyterian minister. *The Cooper Collection of Historic Documents, Cambridge, England.*
Back cover: Typical backcountry log church of the period. *Image by Pubdog*; Portrait of Colonel James Graham. Graham was a hero in the Revolutionary War and an elder in Reverend Craighead's Unity Presbyterian Church. In the Battle of Charlotte, he was wounded nine times and nearly died but was able to crawl to safety. *Wiseman, The North Carolina Portrait Index 1700–1860.*

First published 2014

Manufactured in the United States

ISBN 978.1.62619.542.4

Library of Congress CIP data applied for.

Notice: The information in this book is true and complete to the best of our knowledge. It is offered without guarantee on the part of the author or The History Press. The author and The History Press disclaim all liability in connection with the use of this book.

CONTENTS

PREFACE

In 1976, I moved my family from Connecticut to Charlotte, North Carolina, and was soon visited by my best friend Charles Heywood, who four years previously had moved to Augusta, Georgia. When he arrived at my new home, Chuck said he wanted to take me to a graveyard in Charlotte. I had no idea why he might want to show me a cemetery but politely submitted to his request. He kept his reasons secret until we arrived. We found the graveyard about a half mile from the Sugaw Creek Presbyterian Church in the northeast part of the city. It was obviously an old cemetery, with discolored headstones, grass somewhat overgrown and a rusted decorative iron fence about six feet by ten feet near the front entrance. Within the fence was a single granite stone, which read, "Rev. Alex Craighead. Died March 1766. Monument at cemetery in Charlotte, N.C." Chuck told me that he was a collateral descendant of Reverend Alexander Craighead (he was directly descended from Alexander's brother John Craighead), and he had long wanted to see where his ancestor was buried. I was quite surprised that Chuck had a relative who had lived in the South so long ago. He was from the state of New York, and I was from Massachusetts. We thought of ourselves as Northerners, somewhat out of place in the South.

We then drove to another cemetery near downtown Charlotte and found the monument mentioned on Reverend Craighead's stone. The marker was about twenty feet high and stated that Reverend Alex Craighead was an "Advocate of American Independence from 1743" and an "Inspirer of Mecklenburg Declaration." Chuck explained that his ancestor was a fiery

Scotch-Irish Presbyterian minister who had preached independence from England and was considered the father of the Mecklenburg Declaration of Independence of 1775, the country's first, signed a year before the famous national declaration. I was intrigued with Reverend Craighead and became determined to learn more about his life.

I found that Reverend Craighead wrote a paper in 1743 that upset the royal deputy governor of Pennsylvania, who angrily sent it to the Presbyterian Synod of Philadelphia. The synod denounced the paper, saying it was "full of treason" and "sedition" and "heartily lament[ed] that any man that was ever called a Presbyterian should be guilty of what is in this paper." Reverend Craighead argued that English kings had forfeited their right to rule over America because King Charles II in 1660 reneged on a covenant that made Presbyterianism the official religion of England. As a Scot, Reverend Craighead had many other reasons to hate the English, but by advocating independence from England in 1743, he was twenty years ahead of any known American Revolutionary. Reverend Craighead also told his parishioners that they should resist colonial authorities because these officials were merely extensions of the English Crown. The king of England appointed the royal governor and his council, and the county justices, militia officers and sheriff were all appointed by the governor and his council.

In Mecklenburg County in the foothills of North Carolina, Reverend Craighead was far from the coastal royal governor and free to preach as he wanted. His parishioners included at least 70 percent of the county population and more than one thousand Presbyterian Scotch-Irish. He was a powerful, compelling speaker, and as a result, his parishioners committed early revolutionary acts, including an armed rebellion against the illegal surveying of royal land grantees and the blowing up of a British ammunition wagon train. These defiant actions emboldened settlers in nearby counties to commit rebellious acts against colonial authorities in protest of corruption in the collection of land taxes. Reverend Craighead's parishioners and other counties' settlers then fought the Battle of Alamance, which should be considered the first battle of the Revolutionary War. The same convention that signed the Mecklenburg Declaration of Independence, in which twenty of the twenty-seven delegates were parishioners of Reverend Craighead, also agreed to the Mecklenburg Resolves. The preamble to the Resolves stated that "all Laws and Commissions confirmed by, or derived from the Authority of the King or Parliament, are annulled and vacated." The final test of Reverend Craighead's unique ability to rouse his parishioners on the issue of independence from England came in the Revolutionary War itself. The population of Mecklenburg County in 1775 represented less than 3 percent of the population of North Carolina, but 25 percent of the soldiers from North Carolina who fought in the Revolutionary War were from Mecklenburg, and at least 70 percent of those soldiers were former parishioners of Reverend Craighead. This was further testament to the fiery revolutionary preaching of Alexander Craighead. His story is a fascinating one, and I came to believe that it deserved a much more significant place in history.

ACKNOWLEDGEMENTS

The author acknowledges with profound gratitude Charles Heywood, who was the original inspiration for the book. As a collateral descendant of Reverend Alexander Craighead, Charles first made me aware of his ancestor when I moved to Charlotte, North Carolina, in 1976. He also provided me with an extensive family background on the fiery Presbyterian minister as I began my journey of discovery. Just as importantly, Charles greatly encouraged me during the writing phase of the book and was actively involved with reviewing the manuscript. To my best friend for fifty years, a hearty thank you.

The author wishes to thank Dr. Dan Morrill, professor in the History Department at the University of North Carolina at Charlotte, and his wife, Mary Lynn, for the warm reception they gave Charles Heywood and me in their Charlotte home. Mary Lynn is a direct descendant of Reverend Alexander Craighead and Alexander's son-in-law Reverend David Caldwell. Both Dan and Mary Lynn provided helpful backgrounds on the two Presbyterian ministers, and I frequently referenced Dan's website writings in connection with his position as contributing director of the Charlotte-Mecklenburg Historic Landmarks Commission and his books on the history of Charlotte and Mecklenburg County and the Revolutionary War in the South.

The author thanks Shelia Bumgarner, librarian at the Robinson-Spangler Carolina Room, Charlotte-Mecklenburg Library for permission to use the images of the replica of Mecklenburg County's first courthouse, the

Hezekiah Alexander House and McIntyre's Farm. Thanks also to Sarah E. Koonts, state archivist at the Division of Archives and Records of the North Carolina Department of Cultural Resources, for permission to use the images of Governor William Tryon and the Regulators and the painting of Governor Josiah Martin. My appreciation also goes to Katherine E. Beery, museum registrar at the North Carolina Museum of History, for permission to use the image of the portrait of Reverend David Caldwell. And my gratitude is extended to Matthew Turi, manuscripts research and instruction librarian at the Southern Historical Collection, Wilson Library of the University of North Carolina, for permission to use the image of the rough notes of John McKnitt Alexander from the Charlotte convention of 1775 at which the Mecklenburg Declaration of Independence was signed.

The author's deep gratitude goes to J. Banks Smither, commissioning editor at The History Press, who has been extremely helpful in generating acceptance for the book's concept, knowledgeably clarifying the technological aspects of book production and always ready to help in myriad different ways. Thanks to a very professional commissioning editor.

INTRODUCTION

Friday, May 19, 1775. John Davidson knew he had a three-hour horse ride ahead of him and wanted to get to the Charlotte meeting in plenty of time. Born in Pennsylvania, he had come in 1760 to Mecklenburg County, where, a year later, he married Violet Wilson. Davidson worked as a blacksmith, eking out a living for his wife and six children. Fortunately, his father-in-law had given the couple land on the banks of the Catawba River where they built a two-room log cabin. By noon, Davidson had begun preparing his horse for the long ride. As he did, he thought about the events that had led up to what he suspected would be a dramatic, even fateful convention. Those prospects made him nervous and excited at the same time. The recent past had been tumultuous in Mecklenburg County and throughout the colonies. Using a stiff brush on his shedding horse, Davidson thought about the young men, known as the Mecklenburg Black Boys, who had blown up the British ammunition wagon train in the county just four years before. That had been a daring and dangerous act. He remembered the six Piedmont men the royal governor had hanged four years earlier because they fought against the way the government was run. As he removed dirt, manure and stones from the hooves of the horse, he was reminded of the shocking news three months earlier that the English Parliament had declared the colonies to be in a state of rebellion. Fixing the saddle pad and saddle and then tightening the girth, he thought about the North Carolinians who had formed their own Provincial Congress just a month earlier, a congress that had been severely denounced by the royal governor before he fled to a fort on the Cape Fear River. The forty-year-old Davidson was ready for his long ride. He said goodbye to Violet and the children and rode off to the southeast.

Ephraim Brevard, one of Mecklenburg's first physicians, didn't have to make any ride at all. He lived about three hundred feet from the split-log county courthouse where the meeting was to be held, the courthouse built in 1766 just two years before the incorporation of Charlotte as county seat. Ephraim's future father-in-law, Colonel Thomas Polk, commanding officer of the Mecklenburg militia, had called for the convention to be made up of two delegates selected from each of the Mecklenburg County's militia companies. Brevard was one of those chosen. Born in Maryland around 1744, Brevard lost an eye as a young boy, but that did not prevent him from graduating from the College of New Jersey, now Princeton University, in 1768. He studied medicine in Philadelphia and later in South Carolina. Brevard became a teacher at Queen's College in Charlotte and a delegate to the First North Carolina Provincial Congress. On May 19, at thirty-one years of age, Brevard was still a bachelor. A year later, he married Martha Polk, and their only child, Margaret, was born five years after that. While getting ready for the meeting, Brevard remembered how England's King George III had denied a charter for Queen's College because he feared the school would become a breeding ground for revolution. Despite the king's refusal, the college prospered even without a charter. Brevard also thought about the reports of food shortages in Boston because of the British occupation and about the plans he and other Mecklenburg citizens had made to send one hundred beef cattle to Boston to alleviate the hunger there. In the late afternoon, Ephraim closed his front door and began the short walk to the courthouse.

John McKnitt Alexander, another local resident chosen as a convention delegate, was one of the richest men in Mecklenburg County. He had been born in Maryland in 1733, was self-educated and moved to the foothills of North Carolina around 1754. Once in Mecklenburg County, he worked as a land surveyor, one result of which was personal acquisition of thousands of acres of land. As a large plantation owner, Alexander became even wealthier, raising and selling cotton, and his property grew to over ten miles square. One 1,500-acre parcel, which he named Alexandriana, became Alexander's home. Alexandriana included a large plantation house comfortable enough for his wife, Jane Bain Alexander, and their growing family. A barn, stockyard and still dotted the property. The relative remoteness of his plantation made it a safe place for area men to gather around the spring, sip corn liquor and apple brandy and discuss politics, increasingly the sort that would be viewed by colonial authorities as dangerously radical. About nine miles from Charlotte, Alexandriana would be about a two-hour ride by horse to the courthouse. He would have to leave home nearly as early as John Davidson. As Alexander prepared his favorite horse for the ride south, he, too, thought, as both Davidson and Brevard had, about the increasingly ominous reports from New England, beginning in 1770 with the shocking news of the Boston Massacre and later, in 1773, the equally cheering reports of the Boston Tea Party. News closer to home had recorded the Battle of Alamance in 1771, in which men from Mecklenburg County and neighboring counties had fought against the North Carolina royal governor and his militia over corruption in the government's collection of taxes. Alexander's mind flashed back to the six captured men hanged by the governor after the battle. Political resistance to the British colonial government was dangerous, deadly dangerous. With no little trepidation then, Alexander said goodbye to Jane and the children and headed toward Charlotte.

John Davidson, Dr. Ephraim Brevard and John McKnitt Alexander, with twenty-four other men of Mecklenburg County, finally convened their meeting in the late afternoon of May 19, 1775. Deliberations centered on the grievances held by these men and many of their neighbors concerning the state of their liberties under North Carolina's English-appointed governor. Opinions varied widely, from those delegates holding out for reform and reconciliation with the colonial government, to which they had pledged an oath after the Battle of Alamance, to those advocating more drastic action, repudiation of the oath and a complete break from England. What finally galvanized the delegates to come together in dramatic and unanimous resolve was the arrival at the courthouse of a lone rider with startling news. The rider breathlessly announced that armed fighting had broken out between red-coated British regulars and a ragtag group of patriotic militiamen, first at Lexington and soon after at Concord, Massachusetts. Once again, Americans had died at the hands of the British. For the men of Mecklenburg County convened at the Charlotte courthouse, consensus came quickly. By noon the following day, Saturday, May 20, resolutions of independence written by a committee composed of Dr. Brevard and two others were accepted and signed by all the delegates. What these men had agreed to was the first public pronouncement by Americans resolved to sever ties to the English king who ruled them. Their resolutions came to be known as the Mecklenburg Declaration of Independence. Certainly those brave and determined North Carolinians had experienced enough in their own lives under British authority to lead them to such a dramatic act. Other men in other American colonies, however, surely had similar experiences, experiences that led them to Philadelphia a year later in July 1776. But why had it been only in Mecklenburg County, North Carolina, that twenty-seven men of such varying backgrounds and lives first took the step from which there would be no turning back? The answer is that only in Mecklenburg County had so many men and women come under the influence of a passionate and extraordinary man, a Scotch-Irish Presbyterian minister whom history should honor among those whose lives and words led inexorably to the founding of our American republic. That man was Reverend Alexander Craighead, whose preaching and political agitating in the crucial decades before 1775 made him one of America's first revolutionaries and inspired his parishioners to commit early revolutionary acts, including an armed rebellion against illegal surveying by royal land grantees and the blowing up of a British ammunition wagon train. These acts emboldened settlers in nearby counties to rebel against corrupt government collection of land taxes, leading to the bloody Battle of Alamance. Reverend Craighead's fiery preaching culminated in the convention's agreed upon declaration and his being known as the father of the Mecklenburg Declaration of Independence.

Chapter 1

MECKLENBURG'S FIERY PREACHER

When Reverend Alexander Craighead accepted the call from the Rocky River Presbyterian Church in North Carolina in April 1758, it is likely he was already preaching in its pulpit on a regular basis. He was the first permanent minister of any denomination to preach between the Yadkin River, which runs from about Salisbury down to present-day Rockingham, and the Catawba River, which flows alongside the western boundary of today's Mecklenburg County. At that time, the Rocky River church was in Anson County, but in 1762 the western part of Anson County was split off and became Mecklenburg County. When it was first formed, Mecklenburg was about five times the size that it is now since it extended much farther west, as well as south into what is now South Carolina and north and east into the areas where Concord and Kannapolis are now located.

Reverend Craighead had been a fiery preacher since he first began his ministry in Pennsylvania in 1734. He believed that unless he made his parishioners aware of their sins and convinced them to be reborn with a strong conversion experience, they were damned to hell. He also believed that converted believers could rely on their own inner spirits for guidance. They didn't have to turn to church authorities or to those with more education for answers on how to think or for decisions on their own lives. It led to a more democratic church structure with laypeople having a say in church decisions and theological discussions. Reverend Craighead believed strongly in revivals and was part of America's Great Awakening. The most prominent preacher of the movement was George Whitefield, who first visited America from England in 1739 and had the same theology as Craighead. Whitefield became good friends with both Reverend Craighead and his wife, Agnes, and in his journal of May 13, 1743, Whitefield wrote, "Tuesday. In the morning preached at Wilmington to five thousand; and at Whiteclay Creek in the evening, to three thousand…After sermon at Whiteclay, I rode towards Nottingham with Mr. William Tennent, Mrs. Craghead [*sic*], and with Mr. Blair, all worthy ministers of the Lord Jesus, and with many others belonging to Philadelphia. We rode through the woods singing and praising God."

George Whitefield. *Painting by John Russell, 1770, National Portrait Gallery, London. Courtesy of Wikimedia Commons.*

Reverend Craighead's religious thinking put him at odds with the thinking of the Presbyterian establishment, which believed in a much more traditional approach to church services and theology. One of his confrontations with the Synod of Philadelphia occurred because he went into neighboring church areas and held revivals. Another was over his church rules, which conflicted with those of the synod. In 1743, the long-festering disagreements between Reverend Craighead and other "New Side" ministers with the "Old Side" ministers came to a boiling point. The New Side ministers were expelled from the synod and formed their own presbyteries and synod. By 1753, the synods had reunited, but by that time, the New Side ministers greatly outnumbered the Old Side ministers.

Reverend Craighead was capable of greatly moving his audience. A contemporary Presbyterian minister in Pennsylvania stated that some of Craighead's parishioners would experience emotions so strong during his sermons that they would "burst out with audible noise into bitter crying." Reverend Craighead came by his preaching abilities naturally, as he had descended from a long line of Presbyterian ministers who had preached in the Glasgow area of Scotland. The name Craighead, with the spelling Craighede, which meant "top of the hill," was traced back as far back as 1492. His grandfather Reverend Robert Craighead migrated to Donoughmore,

Ireland, in 1657 and was minister at a church in Londonderry, Ireland, in 1689, when the king of England, James II, tried to massacre the Protestants in Ulster using papal forces. Robert and his family escaped back to Scotland and returned to Ireland after the Scotch-Irish had defeated the English. In 1703, the English Parliament had passed the Test Act, which required all Presbyterian ministers to perform their sacramental services according to the rites of the Anglican Church of England. Most Presbyterian ministers followed their consciences and used the rites of their own church, but that meant that the marriages they performed were illegal, and the children of those marriages were considered bastards. As a Presbyterian minister, Alexander's father, Reverend Thomas Craighead, was threatened with legal proceedings and had no official standing. The sacramental test was a condition of holding civil and military office, and many Presbyterian ministers were forced out of their offices as magistrates. Because of the poor treatment of Presbyterian ministers by the English, Thomas Craighead decided to move his family to America when Alexander was eight years of age, arriving in Boston in 1715. Thomas was a stubborn man, as Alexander turned out to be, and although Reverend Cotton Mather procured Thomas Craighead a position as minister at a Congregational church in Freetown, Massachusetts, the church members went to court to remove him after four years. Even a letter from Reverend Mather couldn't save him.

Most of Reverend Alexander Craighead's parishioners from Windy Cove, Virginia, followed him to the Rocky River area, and like Craighead, they were escaping the dangers of Indian attacks but were also seeking cheaper land in North Carolina. They traveled down the Great Philadelphia Wagon Road, which in 1758 was still not wide enough for wagon travel. Most of the settlers walked to North Carolina with pack animals to carry their supplies and belongings, while Reverend Craighead and his family probably rode on horseback. Starting out from Lexington, Virginia, they rode past Big Lick (now Roanoke) and Rocky Mount, Virginia, and then on to Salem and Salisbury, North Carolina, and arrived just north of present-day Charlotte at Rocky River. The Rocky River church was located in present-day Concord and had been organized years earlier, perhaps as early as 1744, but had only engaged temporary ministers until the arrival of Reverend Craighead.

In November 1758, Reverend Craighead was installed at both the Rocky River church and at the Sugaw Creek church, which was located in the northeast section of present-day Charlotte. The Sugaw Creek church was formed in 1755 but also didn't have a permanent minister until Reverend Craighead's arrival. The installation services were conducted by a young

Great Philadelphia Wagon Road. *Illustration by author.*

Presbyterian minister named Reverend William Richardson, who was traveling through the area on horseback as part of a missionary tour to the Cherokee Nation. When Richardson arrived at Reverend Craighead's new home, he was introduced to the family, which then included Craighead's new wife, Jane, whom he married after his wife, Agnes, died; six daughters: Margaret (twenty-three), Mary (twenty-two), Agnes Nancy (eighteen), Rachel (sixteen), Jane (fifteen) and Elizabeth (ten); and two sons, Robert (seven) and Thomas (five). Reverend Richardson's missionary work never occurred because of the breakout of hostilities with the Cherokee Indians, but this allowed him time to get to know Agnes Nancy Craighead, fall in love and marry her the following year. Both churches held their installation services on Monday, November 6, 1758. On the day before, Reverend Richardson preached at the Rocky River church and rode five miles on horseback, giving notice of the next day's installation. On that Sunday, Reverend Craighead preached at the Sugaw Creek church and rode twenty miles on horseback to preach to settlers who were in the process of organizing a new church. These settlers were likely the parishioners in the Steele Creek area, who formed a church just two years later, in 1760. At the time Reverend Craighead began preaching to that congregation, the services were likely in a temporary structure consisting of four upright logs holding up a roof made of split logs and branches for protection from the weather. These "churches" were typically about eight feet by twelve feet and contained a few roughly hewn benches. Presbyterian ministers had to travel many miles on horseback preaching to outlying congregations in addition to their permanent pastorates. They also made long trips to visit parishioners and call on the sick and dying. These outlying congregations of Craighead became organized churches over the next eight years, usually by erecting a log church, starting with the Steele Creek church on the east side of present-day Charlotte in 1760; the Hopewell church, northeast of present-day Charlotte in present-day Huntersville (originally called Craighead after Reverend Craighead) in 1762; the Poplar Tent church, in present-day south Concord in 1764; the Centre church in present-day Mooresville, north of present-day Charlotte in 1765; and the Providence church in present-day south Charlotte in 1766. Mecklenburg County in 1766 was about twice as large as its present size since Cabarrus County and Union County had not yet been split off into separate counties. Reverend Craighead initially began preaching to the Providence settlers from a large rock, which can still be found near the present church building, until the parishioners were able to build a log cabin structure. Reverend Craighead also served as a missionary minister to the Presbyterian gathering at Clear Creek in Mecklenburg County, which became the Philadelphia Presbyterian Church in present-day Mint Hill in 1770 and to the Unity Presbyterian Church (founded in 1764) in nearby Tryon County. The church is in present-day Catawba Springs in that part of Tryon County, which became Lincoln County in 1779. In 1764, Reverend Craighead bought 551 acres of land on Long Creek, which was located about five miles north of the Sugaw Creek church. His other churches were ten to twenty miles by horseback from his home.

When Reverend Alexander Craighead preached, he wore a Geneva gown with a cassock underneath, just as his father, Thomas, had. The Geneva gown was a black, flowing, ankle-length robe with double-bell sleeves. It

Log church. *Photo by Pubdog. Courtesy of Wikimedia Commons.*

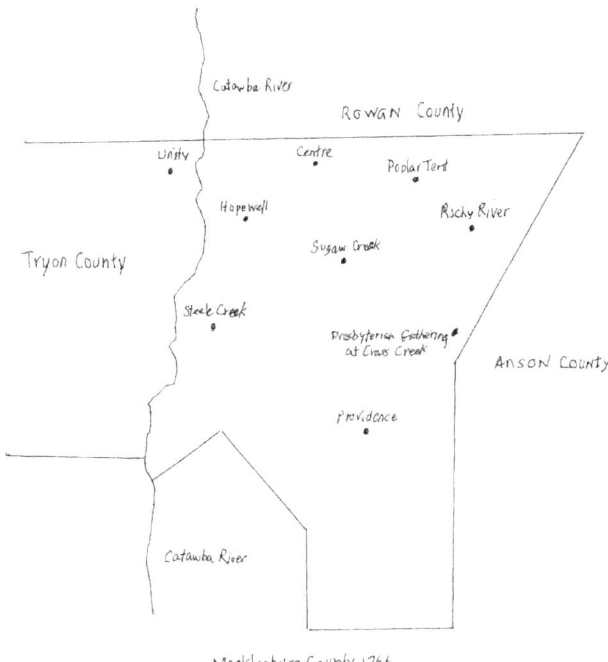

Reverend Alexander Craighead's churches (1766). *Illustration by author.*

was named after the garment that John Calvin wore when he preached in the sixteenth century in Geneva, Switzerland. The robe had velvet panels running over the neck and down both sides of the front. It was usually left open in the front, revealing the cassock underneath. The cassock was a tighter, non-flowing, ankle-length garment with black buttons from top to bottom, sometimes thirty-three in number, representing the years of the life of Jesus. It also had white tabs hanging from the neck to about the mid-chest. Reverend Craighead wore the Geneva gown only when he was giving a sermon, not on other occasions.

For most of the parishioners of Reverend Craighead's churches, Sunday was a long day. It was also a very important day to them. They arose early in the morning, milked the cows, had breakfast and packed lunches. They hitched up teams of horses to wagons and put quilts in the wagon beds for the children and chairs for the adults. In order to make the 10:00 a.m. service, they had to leave early. Many families rode over two hours each way to attend services. When the morning service of two hours or more was completed, the families spread out their lunches on rocks to be used as tables. After lunch, they went back into the church for another service that also lasted for two hours or more. Not only were the Scotch-Irish religious, but the sermons also appealed to their minds. Although they typically couldn't read, they still understood the theological points that Reverend Craighead was making. They believed that their very souls were in jeopardy. They also believed that their relationship with God was dependent on their understanding Reverend Craighead's message. The sermons were relevant to their lives and critically important to them. After the services, the parishioners returned home to milk the cows a second time and retire for the night. They often talked to other parishioners during the week to discuss what the sermon had meant. Craighead's sermons provided them with a means of stimulating their minds that wasn't otherwise available to them. The fact that most of them were illiterate didn't slow their inquisitiveness. Reverend Craighead's sermons were a bright spot in the weekly lives of his parishioners. From a theological standpoint, the typical Scotch-Irish Presbyterian believed that God would reward the believer for his hard work and good works, both in this life and in the life hereafter. He expected God to favor him in his battles with Indians, and he believed that the only good Indian was a dead Indian. He also believed that God had assigned him the job of killing as many Indians as possible.

As was true of Reverend Craighead's parishioners in Pennsylvania and Virginia, the North Carolina backcountry settlers were almost exclusively

Reverend Alexander Craighead. *Ink drawing by Jean Plumer.*

farmers. They weren't plantation owners like the farmers on the east coast of North Carolina. Their farms were relatively small. Over three-quarters of the backcountry farms were between one hundred and five hundred acres of land, while 5 percent were over one thousand acres and 5 percent were under one hundred acres. The number of settlers in Mecklenburg County grew rapidly in the time that Reverend Craighead preached there from 1758 to his death in 1766. A survey done by Governor Arthur Dobbs in 1755, before Reverend Craighead came to North Carolina, showed that there were 97 families, of which 75 were Scotch-Irish, in the area that became Mecklenburg County. Another survey showed that Scotch-Irish families on average had 2 parents and 7 children at that time, so the total population in the county would have been about 870 that year. A survey in March

1765 showed 150 families in the county or about 1,350 people. In 1767, the Governor's Council reported that there were "1,600 white inhabitants in Mecklenburg County," and they were "mostly Presbyterians." That means that the population in Mecklenburg County almost doubled from 1755 to 1767, approximately the time that Reverend Craighead preached there. It is estimated from the total number of churches in the county in 1766 (seven Presbyterian churches of Reverend Craighead, two Lutheran and one Baptist) that about 70 percent of the population attended Reverend Craighead's churches with about 1,100 Scotch-Irish parishioners. Because Reverend Craighead was such a powerful and persuasive preacher and he had a great majority of Mecklenburg's residents as his parishioners, he exerted a tremendous influence over the thinking within the county.

There was another important subject on which Reverend Craighead preached, and that was independence from England. When Reverend Craighead was preaching at the Middle Octorara Presbyterian Church in Lancaster County, Pennsylvania, which was about fifty miles west of Philadelphia, he was president of the Covenanter Society in Pennsylvania from 1743 to 1749. In his first year, he gathered all the members of the society at his Middle Octorara church, and with drawn swords, they renewed their oaths to the National Covenant and the Solemn League and Covenant. As part of the ceremony, the Covenanters adopted these words:

> *We do likewise enter our Testimony against George the I, his having any legal Right to rule over this Realm, because he being an outlandish Lutheran; likewise against George the II for their being sworn Prelaticks, the head of Malignants, and Protector of Sectarian Hereticks, and Electory Princes of Brunswick, in chusing* [sic] *of New Emperers, which is their giving their Power to the Beast; and for their Confederacy with Popish Princes, directly contrary to the Second Commandment; and for their want of Spiritual and National Qualifications, as is above said; and for their being established Head of Church by the laws of England.*

To the Covenanters, the idea that covenanting was an integral part of Presbyterian church doctrine went hand in hand with the concept that the king of England had no right to rule over America. In 1560, the Scottish Parliament declared Presbyterianism the official religion of Scotland and abolished the rule of the pope and outlawed the celebration of the Roman Catholic Mass. In 1581, Roman Catholics in Scotland made a strong push to regain dominance in the country, and the General Assembly of the

King George II of England. *Painting by Thomas Hudson, 1744, National Portrait Gallery, London. Courtesy of Wikimedia Commons.*

Presbyterian Church adopted the National Covenant, which again denounced the pope and the doctrines of the Roman Catholic Church. In 1638, the General Assembly adopted the Solemn League and Covenant, which reiterated the terms of the National Covenant and requested each member make an oath to maintain Presbyterianism as the official religion of Scotland. The Scottish Parliament adopted the Solemn League and Covenant in 1640 and required all Scottish citizens to subscribe to it. The Solemn League and Covenant was agreed to by the English Parliament in 1643 in exchange for a promise from the Presbyterian Covenanters that they would aid the English in their war against papists in Catholic Ireland. With the agreement, the Scottish Presbyterian system of church government was adopted for England. The English Parliament agreement also decreed that Presbyterianism was the only true doctrine taught in the Bible. This was reversed seventeen years later in 1660, when the Stuarts came back into power in England and Charles II took the throne. The Covenant was disowned, Anglicanism was again made the Established Church of England, and the king was declared the "Defender of the Faith." Reverend Craighead preached that the king, by breaking a covenant made with God and replacing it with false and popish Anglican doctrine, had lost his right to rule.

King Charles II of England. *Painting by John Michael Wright, 1660–1665, National Portrait Gallery, London. Courtesy of Wikimedia Commons.*

Sometime before May 1743, a paper was published anonymously but widely attributed to Reverend Craighead. There is no copy of this paper still in existence, but from the reaction the paper received, it can be assumed that it went further in denouncing the king and his right to rule than any of his previous pamphlets, which had been printed by Benjamin Franklin. The paper was shown to Deputy Governor George Thomas of Pennsylvania and, in his name, was presented to the Synod of Philadelphia. Reverend Craighead had earlier run-ins with the synod and two years prior had withdrawn from the synod and formed a new presbytery with ministers whose thinking was more in keeping with his own. The synod listened to a reading of the paper on May 25, 1743, and made the following ruling:

> [I]*t was unanimously agreed: That is it full of treason, sedition, and distraction, and grievous perverting of the sacred oracles to the ruin of all societies and civil government…and we hereby unanimously, with the greatest sincerity, declare that we detest this paper, and with it all principles and practices that tend to destroy the civil and religious rights of mankind, or to foment or encourage sedition or dissatisfaction with the civil government that we are now under, or rebellion, treason, or any thing that is disloyal. And if Mr. Alexander Craighead be the author we know nothing of the matter. And we hereby declare, that he hath been no member of our society for some time past, nor do we acknowledge him as such though we cannot but heartily lament that any man that was ever called a Presbyterian should be guilty of what is in this paper.*

This was twenty years before any known revolutionary in America began to argue for independence from England. Thomas Paine was only six, Patrick Henry was seven, James Otis Jr. was eighteen and Samuel Adams was just graduating with a master's degree from Harvard. Reverend Craighead believed that the king of England had forfeited his right to rule, that all people are equal in the eyes of God and that the democratic structure of the Presbyterian Church lent itself as a model for an American government. These beliefs led him to preach for an independent democratic America. This was combined with his intense hatred of England brought on by the religious persecutions that his father, Reverend Thomas Craighead, and other Presbyterian ministers had endured from the English in Ireland; the fact that the king of England, James II, had tried to massacre all the Protestants in Ulster in 1689 and his grandfather Reverend Robert Craighead had to escape to Scotland; and the over one thousand years of wars the Scots fought with the English. All these reasons led him to publish his 1743 paper affirming his revolutionary thinking. It is likely that his advocacy for independence actually started when he first began preaching nine years earlier.

In 1744, Reverend Craighead published a pamphlet printed by Benjamin Franklin entitled *Renewal of the Covenants, National and Solemn League*, in which he explained the importance of the National Covenant and Solemn League and Covenant and the critical nature of confessing one's sins and acting on one's moral responsibilities. Like prior pamphlets, he also denounced the rulers of England with these words:

> *We lift up our Testimony against Charles the I his conduct in maintaining of a War in Opposition to the carrying on of the Work of Reformation...* [Charles I, the king of England, Scotland, and Ireland from 1625 to 1645, fought against the reformation movement by moving the Church of England away from Calvinism and toward Roman Catholicism.]
>
> *We do testify against the Motion made by Cromwell to the General Assembly of the Church of Scotland...* [Oliver Cromwell was first lord protector of the commonwealth. When the Scots proclaimed Charles II as their rightful king, he appealed to the General Assembly of the Church of Scotland to see the error in its alliance with Charles II. The General Assembly didn't change its position. Cromwell then invaded Scotland, killing four thousand Scottish soldiers and capturing ten thousand in taking Edinburgh.]
>
> *We do testify against the Conduct of Charles the II in making Application to the Parliament, for Liberty to read the Service-Book in his own Family... and made a Speech to the Parliament to this Purpose...* [Charles II reigned from 1660 to 1685. Soon after he became king, the English Parliament returned the Church of England to Anglican dominance, made the Anglican Book of Common Prayer compulsory and prohibited religious assemblies of more than five people, unless under the auspices of the Church of England.]

RENEWAL
OF THE
COVENANTS,
National and Solemn League;
A Confession of Sins; and Engagement to Duties;
AND A
TESTIMONY;
As they were carried out at Middle Octarara in *Pennſlvania*, November 11, 1743.
TOGETHER WITH
An Introductory PREFACE.
Re-printed in the YEAR MDCCXLVIII.

Renewal of the Covenants pamphlet. *Pamphlet cover illustration by author.*

> *We do also testify against James Duke of York his having any legal Right to rule over this Realm, by Reason of his Popish Principles: Likewise we join our Testimony given against the Duke of York's abominable Anti-Christian Toleration by that faithful Minister and Martyr of Jesus Christ, Mr. James Renwick.* [James, Duke of York, was king of England as James II and king of Scotland as James VII from 1685 to 1688. James Renwick was a Scottish Presbyterian minister and Covenanter who spent five years preaching throughout Scotland. He was hunted down by the king's troopers, captured in 1688 and ordered to swear loyalty to the king. He refused and was hanged in Edinburgh. His head and hands were severed and attached to the gates of the city.]

The actions of all four of these English rulers only added to Reverend Craighead's dislike of England and his rejection of the English king's right to govern America. Reverend Craighead's fiery sermons and papers led historian Charles A. Hanna to write in 1902 in his book about the Scotch-Irish, "Mr. Craighead was the foremost American of his day in advocating those principles of civil liberty under a republican form of government, to confirm which the Revolutionary War was fought."

Even when Reverend Craighead moved to the Windy Cove Presbyterian Church in the Shenandoah Valley, Virginia, in 1749, he was not able to preach freely. He was farther from the royal coastal authorities, but there was an Anglican church in Augusta County. Two vestrymen of the church testified before the Governor's Council of Virginia that "the Rev. Alexander Creaghead [*sic*] has taught and maintained treasonable positions, and preached and published pernicious doctrines." On June 10, 1752, Lieutenant Governor Robert Dinwiddie ordered the sheriff of Augusta County to "apprehend and secure in custody the said Creaghead, and immediately bring him before the Governor in Williamsburg." Having heard beforehand that the vestrymen were about to make the charges, Reverend Craighead went to Philadelphia in May 1752 and was given letters of recommendation by two ministers in the synod of Philadelphia. He also received a letter from Governor James Hamilton of Pennsylvania, which stated that the ministers' letters were certified. When Craighead returned to Windy Cove on August 21, 1752, his friend and neighbor Richard Woods, one of the magistrates in Augusta County, repeated the administration of the oath, including the test and thirty-nine articles, except what was exempted by the Act of Toleration. The Governor's Council met on October 17, 1752, and Reverend Craighead appeared before the body and answered the complaints against him and produced the ministers' letters and the Pennsylvania governor's certificate. The council ordered "that the said Alexander Creaghead be permitted to preach, upon fully recanting his disloyal Principles, and the Doctrines contained in the Book delivered to the Governor, and taking the Oaths to the Government openly to the General Court."

Lieutenant Governor Robert Dinwiddie of Virginia. *Painting by unknown artist, National Portrait Gallery, London. Courtesy of Wikimedia Commons.*

Reverend Craighead had escaped being arrested and was able to resume preaching in his Windy Cove church.

In 1756, Reverend Craighead's wife of twenty-two years and mother of his eight children, Agnes, died at the age of forty-one. She was buried at the Windy Cove church with Alexander conducting the service. Reverend Craighead attended a presbytery meeting on January 25, 1758, at which he was asked to visit churches on a southern trip to Meherrin in Virginia and Nutbush and Rocky River in North Carolina. It was on this trip that he formed a close relationship with the parishioners at the Rocky River church in Mecklenburg County. Life in Virginia had become intolerable, as he and his parishioners were forced to defend themselves from regular Indian attacks that began after General Braddock's defeat at the French Fort Duquesne (present-day Pittsburg) in Pennsylvania in the summer of 1755 during the French and Indian War. Rachel, one of Reverend Craighead's daughters, later described how close the family's escape was on one occasion, writing, "As they went out at one door the Indians came in at the other." Reverend Craighead found that he couldn't preach freely in Augusta County, which was controlled by the local Anglican Church. He was also burdened by the fact that he had to pay taxes to support the Anglican Church and that, for a long time, he wasn't allowed to conduct the rites of matrimony for his parishioners. When he was presented with a call from the members of the Rocky River church in Mecklenburg County, North Carolina, by the Hanover Presbytery on April 26, 1758, he gladly accepted.

In Mecklenburg County, in the foothills of North Carolina, he was far from the royal coastal authorities, and there were no Anglican churches anywhere in the area. He had finally found his haven. In *Sketches of North Carolina*, Reverend William Henry Foote wrote in 1846:

> *In Carolina, he found a people remote from the seat of authority, among whom the intolerant laws were a dead letter, so far divided from other congregations, even of his own faith or practice; so united in general principles of religion and church government, that he was the teacher of the whole population, and here his spirit rested. Here he passed his days; here he poured forth his principles of religious and civil government, undisturbed by the jealousy of the government, too distant to be aware of his doings, or too careless to be interested in the poor and distant emigrants on the Catawba. Mr. Craighead had the privilege of forming the principles, both civil and religious, in no measured degree, of a race of man that feared God, and feared not labor and hardship, or the face of man; a race that sought freedom and property in the wilderness, and having found them, rejoiced,—a race capable of great excellence, mental and physical, whose minds could conceive the glorious idea of Independence.*

Reverend Craighead was finally able to preach freely, using his great oratory skills to promote independence from England. In addition to preaching freedom from Great Britain, he also advocated resistance to the local colonial authorities. He reasoned that the colonial authorities were merely extensions of the English Crown since the Crown appointed the North Carolina royal governor and his council and the governor and his council appointed the county justices, militia officers and the sheriff.

In addition to all his pastoral duties at the seven churches, Reverend Craighead also found time to teach school to his congregations' children. Soon after he arrived, he founded the Sugaw Creek Academy in a log cabin schoolhouse next to the site of the present Sugaw Creek church. A brick academy building, which still stands, was built on the same ground in 1837. One young boy who attended Sugaw Creek Academy and was taught by Reverend Craighead was William Lee Davidson. Davidson became a brigadier general for the Patriots during the Revolutionary War, and Davidson College and the town of Davidson, North Carolina, were named after him. The amount of schooling the Scotch-Irish children typically received during those years was extremely minimal. Even in the early 1800s, the records of one North Carolina county showed that only

10 percent of the white school-age children were enrolled in schools. The children were receiving only about 1.5 years of education on average. The lack of education was demonstrated in the inability of the adults to write. A study of one Piedmont County's wills in the 1700s showed that only a little over 50 percent of the property owners could write, based on those who signed their names and those who only made their marks. This was typical of backcountry Scotch-Irish settlements. Levels of schooling were much lower than in the other areas of the country. The Anglican missionary Charles Woodmason, who was sent to America to convert Presbyterians and Baptists to Anglicanism and Indians to Christianity, wrote in his journal, "Few can read—fewer can write…these people despise knowledge." There were no schools like New England's town schools or Virginia's parish schools. Charles Woodmason also wrote, "Through the nonestablishment of public schools, a great multitude of children are now grown up, in the greatest ignorance of ev'ry thing save vice—in which they are adepts."

Presbyterian academies, such as Sugaw Creek Academy, attempted to fill the void, but even those academies were few and far between and were designed primarily to prepare young men for the ministry and to educate the elite. Most of these academies were small, struggled greatly and didn't typically survive more than a few years. The Sugaw Creek Academy not only survived but also prospered due to the strong will of Reverend Craighead. He had a special skill when it came to handling the Scotch-Irish boys.

Schoolhouse from the 1700s. *Illustration from* Pictorial Fieldbook of the Revolution, *1850, by Benson J. Lossing. Courtesy of Wikimedia Commons.*

When Reverend Craighead came to North Carolina, the law in the colony, based on the Marriage Act, was that only ministers of the Church of England could perform the rite of marriage. The law did allow civil authorities to conduct marriages, but only if the county had no Anglican pastor. If Reverend Craighead's parishioners chose to be married by a Mecklenburg civil authority in addition to Reverend Craighead performing the wedding, this meant an extra economic burden. The Scotch-Irish generally ignored the law, and Reverend Craighead, like other Presbyterian ministers in the foothills of North Carolina, performed many marriage ceremonies. But the question always remained of whether the children would be considered bastards and whether an inheritance will would be found legal in the courts.

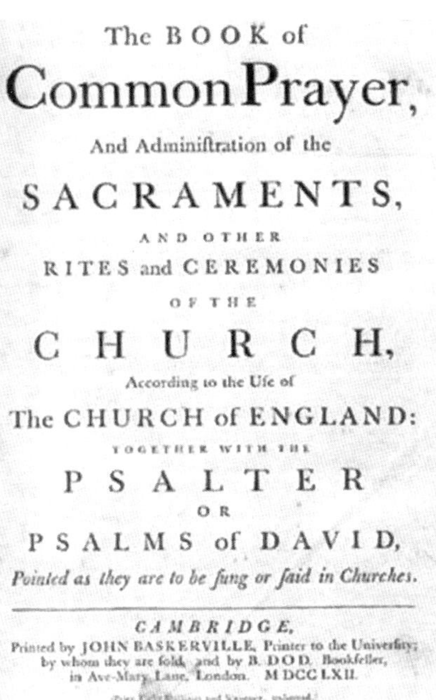
The BOOK of
Common Prayer,
And Adminiſtration of the
SACRAMENTS,
AND OTHER
RITES and CEREMONIES
OF THE
CHURCH,
According to the Uſe of
The CHURCH of ENGLAND:
TOGETHER WITH THE
PSALTER
OR
PSALMS of DAVID,
Pointed as they are to be ſung or ſaid in Churches.

CAMBRIDGE,
Printed by JOHN BASKERVILLE, Printer to the Univerſity; by whom they are ſold, and by B. DOD, Bookſeller, in Ave-Mary Lane, London. MDCCLXII.

Anglican Book of Common Prayer. Printed by John Baskerville, 1762. *Courtesy of Wikimedia Commons.*

Scotch-Irish weddings in the backcountry were unusual affairs. Banns or public announcements of impending weddings were posted at Reverend Craighead's church and other Presbyterian churches on two consecutive Sundays to ensure that there wasn't bigamy involved. The groom also gave a marriage bond, swearing that there was no lawful reason to prevent the marriage, and at least two witnesses swore to its truthfulness. Wedding invitations were given out at the church and were often open invitations. Friends and relatives came to the home of the bride the day before the wedding with homemade gifts. On the wedding day, friends of the groom headed toward the church on horseback and stopped at cabins along the way, shooting off their rifles and passing around a bottle of whiskey. They were opposed by friends of the bride, who were also armed with rifles. The bride's friends cut down trees along the path, created blockades of vines and branches and fired off volleys with their rifles. The two groups then met and had a contest of racing their horses for a bottle of whiskey wrapped in ribbons. The more the route was blocked with logs and brush, the more they could show off their tenacity and horsemanship. Whoever won the whiskey bottle passed it around to all the participants with a great deal of whooping and hollering. There were also contests of wrestling, running, jumping and even gander pulling among the men. After the fun on the route to the wedding, the groups then met at the church with the other invited guests, if it was a "bidden wedding." When neighbors and kin weren't invited, they took out their revenge by cutting off the manes and tails on the horses of the wedding party. The bride was ushered into the church by the best man, rather than her father, to stand in front of Reverend Craighead at the altar. During the wedding, the bride and groom put their right hands behind their backs. Then the gloves on those hands were removed by the best man and the bridesmaid simultaneously, allowing the rings to be placed later on their fingers.

After Reverend Craighead conducted the ceremony, there were more rifles shot into the air and much yelling, kissing and drinking. Then a dance was held with jigs and reels to the sounds of a fiddle. Before dinner, a game was played of mock abduction where the bride was "stolen" by the groom's friends and "rescued" by the bride's friends. The bride's parents provided the wedding feast with great quantities of food and drinks. At the dinner, the groomsmen tried to steal the bride's shoe under the table, while the bridesmaids tried to stop them. If the shoe was successfully stolen, the bride couldn't dance until it was found. Also during the dinner, "Black Betty," a bottle of whiskey, was passed among the wedding guests, and each man held the bottle high and toasted, "Here's to the bride, thumping luck and big children." It was important to have big children to grow into big men as fighters and big women as workers. After the dinner, the maids would dress the bride for bed, and she would pretend to be shy and run away, only to be dragged back by the maids. Before entering the bedroom of their new home, the bride and groom would pretend they didn't want to go in and would struggle fiercely before being forced into the bed. The wedding party then surrounded the bed and gave lewd advice. The bridesmaids threw a rolled-up stocking over their shoulders at the bride, and the groomsmen did the same at the groom. The first one to hit the target was considered the next to marry. The wedding party then serenaded the couple from outside the house with rifle firings, bells and whistles. The next morning, a bottle of whiskey was brought to the bride and groom, and the fun continued, sometimes for days.

In addition to the Marriage Act of North Carolina, which stipulated that only Anglican ministers could perform the rite of marriage, Reverend

Bishop of London certificate. *The Cooper Collection of Historical Documents, Cambridge, England. Courtesy of Wikimedia Commons.*

Craighead had other reasons to resist the North Carolina government. The Vestry Act required all settlers to pay taxes to support the Anglican Church. The act also gave Anglicans dominion over education by declaring that no schoolmaster could "keep school…without the license of the Lord Bishop of London." This presented Reverend Craighead's Presbyterian parishioners with a tremendous economic burden.

In 1760, two years after Reverend Craighead became the pastor of the Rocky River church, a problem arose with two of the elders of the church. They were Robert Harris and Nathaniel Alexander, who later became governor of North Carolina in 1805. For the previous two years, Craighead had fervently preached to the Rocky River parishioners of the need for independence from England and resistance to the colonial government. Soon after Reverend Craighead's arrival in North Carolina, the colonial authorities became very aggressive in the collection of land taxes. There was also a lot of corruption involved in this collection. Sheriffs would overcharge for the amount of land taxes due and deliberately lose tax records and claim a settler hadn't paid his taxes, when in fact he had. Many of the Scotch-Irish settlers in the area that would become Mecklenburg County in 1762 told the North Carolina agents who attempted to collect taxes that their land was in South Carolina. If the North Carolina and South Carolina border dispute were resolved, it would greatly aid the colonial authorities in collecting taxes, but it would be detrimental to the area's settlers. When Nathaniel Alexander and Robert Harris agreed to serve on a commission to settle the boundary line, Reverend Craighead officially "resigned" from the Rocky River church in the summer of 1760 because of its cooperation with the North Carolina authorities. This was actually a symbolic gesture because he continued to preach in the church and serve the community until his death.

On December 11, 1762, the North Carolina Assembly voted to make the western part of Anson County a separate area called Mecklenburg County. The county was named in honor of king of England George III's wife, Charlotte, who came from a small town in Germany called Mecklenburg-Strelitz, and Charlotte was later also named in her honor. The bill to have a separate Mecklenburg County was accompanied by a petition from several settlers in Anson County and was strongly supported by Nathaniel Alexander, elder of the Rocky River church. On December 31, the Governor's Council appointed sixteen men to be His Majesty's justices of the peace for Mecklenburg County: Alexander Lewis, Nathaniel Alexander, John Thomas, Robert McClenahan, Paul Barringer, Henry Foster, Robert Miller, Robert Harris, Richard Barry, Martin Phifer, Robert Ramsey, James

Society for the Propagation of the Gospell in Foreign Parts Seal 1704. *Society's collections, Lambeth Palace Library, London. Courtesy of Wikimedia Commons.*

Robinson, Matthew Floyd, Abraham Alexander, Thomas Polk and James Patton. Most of these men were parishioners in Reverend Craighead's churches. Then, on February 26, 1763, Moses Alexander was appointed high sheriff and Robert Harris was made clerk of court and register of deeds.

In an attempt to counter the tremendous influence of Reverend Alexander Craighead, Governor Arthur Dobbs of North Carolina requested in 1764 that England's Society for the Propagation of the Gospell in Foreign Parts send an Anglican minister or schoolmaster to Mecklenburg County. The minister chosen for this purpose was Reverend Andrew Morton, and he arrived in Wilmington in 1765, the year of the Stamp Act. He got as far as Cape Fear, decided not to go on to Mecklenburg County and reported on his reasons for not doing so to the secretary of the society:

> *Reverend Doctor,*
> *I wrote to you in June last informing you of my Journey to my new mission in Mecklenburg County—From Newbern I pursued my Journey to Cape Fear where I received such Intelligence as discouraged me from proceeding any further—There I was well informed that the inhabitants of Mecklenburg are entire dissenters of the most rigid kind—That they had a solemn league and covenant teacher* [Rev. Alexander Craighead] *among them. That they were in general greatly adverse to the Church of England—and they looked upon a law* [the Vestry Act] *lately enacted in this province for the better establishment of the Church as oppressive as the Stamp Act and were determined to prevent it taking place there, by opposing the settlement of any minister of the Church of England that might be sent amongst them—In short it was very evident that in Mecklenburg County I could be of little use to the honorable Society and I thought it but prudent to decline embroiling*

King George III of England. *Painting by Allan Ramsay, 1761–1762, National Portrait Gallery, London. Courtesy of Wikimedia Commons.*

> *myself with an infatuated people of no purpose and trusting the Venerable Society, upon a just representation of the matter would not be dissatisfied with my conduct.*

Reverend Craighead had such a hold on his parishioners it is unlikely that the Anglican minister Reverend Morton would have caused any changes in the thinking of the Scotch-Irish settlers if he had come to Mecklenburg County.

There were many funerals conducted by Reverend Craighead during his time in Mecklenburg County. Rates of death in the southern backcountry were higher than in the colonies to the north. There were deaths not only from the violent attacks of Indians but also from the violence among the Scotch-Irish themselves. The biggest killer was malaria, but people also died from milk sickness. Cattle that grazed in the woods ate white snakeroot plant, which contained a poison that contaminated the milk and meat. The Scotch-Irish had unusual funeral customs, which they brought with them from the Scottish lowlands and Ireland. As a man or woman was dying, he or she was gently lifted from the bed and laid on the floor to put the spirit close to the earth's forces. The dead body was then placed on a board and closely observed by kin and friends. A plate of salt and dirt, unmixed, was then put on the dead body's chest. The salt represented the spirit, and the dirt stood for the flesh. Everybody in the neighborhood came to visit—even enemies—and they all touched the body. Foul play was often suspected, and there was a belief that if a murderer touched the victim's body, it would start to bleed.

After the deathwatch, the family held a wake, which came from the Scottish word "LikeWake." The closest neighbors all stopped working until the burial, all the dishes and utensils were removed from the shelves and drawers, mirrors were covered or taken down, clocks were stopped and the dials of clocks were covered. The wake lasted for one or two days. Reverend Craighead would read scriptures, say prayers and deliver a psalm. Guests were provided with pipes and tobacco and served spirits of whiskey and brandy. Drinking was typically very heavy. After the wake, a funeral was conducted by Reverend Craighead at the burial site. The number of people attending the funeral was typically quite large. Every relative, no matter how distant a kin, was expected to attend without regard to the age or character of the deceased, as long as the distance traveled was reasonable. The body, usually wrapped in a cloth sack because coffins were too expensive, was carried to the place of burial with a procession following. The procession sometimes was between a quarter mile and a half mile long. The funeral service usually consisted of prayers said by Reverend Craighead and, on rare occasions, included a sermon. When the burial was concluded, the assembled mourners returned to the house of the deceased for food, drinks and entertainment. Small cakes called "arval bread" were given out and considered a parting gift from the deceased. Funerals were expensive for the deceased's family, and it was important that it be done right, so directions were often included in the deceased's will. Although Scotch-Irish Presbyterians were concerned with salvation like the Puritans in New England, they weren't obsessed with it as they were in the North. The primary concern of the Scotch-Irish was to have courage in the face of death, as well as the violence and uncertainty of life.

Some of Reverend Craighead's favorite activities were the visits that he and other leading men of Mecklenburg County made to the cotton plantation of John McKnitt Alexander. It was about three miles north of his home on Long Creek, which was a relatively short horseback ride compared to the ten- to twenty-mile rides to most of his churches. Alexander's homestead was on a parcel of land he called Alexandriana, which was just one part of the thousands of acres of land he owned. In addition to growing and selling cotton, he also made a lucrative living as a surveyor. John McKnitt Alexander was an elder in Craighead's Hopewell church, located about five miles to the west of Alexandriana. The men spent their time there involved in long discussions about the events of the day and politics. Included among the men were Dr. Ephraim Brevard, a physician; Hezekiah Alexander, a large plantation owner, county magistrate, an elder in the Hopewell church and a brother of John McKnitt; Waightstill Avery, a lawyer and a border in the house of Hezekiah Alexander; and Abraham Alexander, a surveyor and justice of the peace, an elder in the Sugaw Creek church with a home about ten miles south of the church and a first cousin of John McKnitt and Hezekiah. They sat on logs at a spring on the plantation and drank potent drinks, such as corn liquor and apple brandy, which John McKnitt distilled on his property. It was reported that Reverend Craighead was able to keep up with his parishioners and friends in their ability to consume liquor and that when he entertained, he served something other than Presbyterian punch in his elegant punch bowl and glasses. Reverend Craighead used the meetings as an opportunity to expound on his ideas about independence from England and resistance to unfair colonial laws.

Reverend Craighead was one-half of the combination that was to produce tremendous early revolutionary activity in Mecklenburg County. The other half of the combination was his Scotch-Irish parishioners. The long inbred culture of the Scotch-Irish was the perfect complement to Reverend Craighead's fiery preaching.

Chapter 2

REVEREND CRAIGHEAD'S FEROCIOUS PARISHIONERS

The reputation of the Scotch-Irish as ferocious fighters was well earned. As far back as AD 71, the future Scots, known then as Celts, showed the Romans their fighting spirit. At that time, the Romans had conquered most of future England, and they were attempting to advance to the north and conquer what became the lowlands of Scotland. The Roman historian Cassius Dio provided a vivid description of these Celtic people:

> *They dwell in tents, naked and unshod, possess their women in common, and in common rear all their offspring. Their form of rule is democratic for the most part, and they are very fond of plundering; consequently they choose their boldest men as rulers. They go into battle in chariots, and have small swift horses; there are also foot soldiers, very swift in running and very firm in standing their ground. For arms they have a shield and short spear, with a bronze apple attached to the end of the spear shaft so that when it is shaken it may clash and terrify the enemy; and they also have a dagger. They can endure hunger and cold and any kind of hardship; for they plunge into the swamps and exist there for many days with only their heads above water, and in the forests they support themselves upon barks and roots, and for all emergencies they prepare a certain kind of food, the eating of a small portion of which, the size of a bean, prevents them from feeling either hunger or thirst.*

The Romans never were able to defeat the lowlanders. In AD 122, Roman emperor Hadrian gave up trying and built a seven-hundred-mile wall from sea to sea that bears his name. The purpose of the wall was to prevent the Celtic lowlanders from gaining back the lands the Romans had been able to win. The wall eventually became the rough dividing line between Scotland and England. There followed almost constant wars between the natives occupying these two areas of land. Prior to the establishment of Scotland and England in the ninth and tenth centuries, the areas witnessed battles between the Picts/Dal Riatans and the Northumbia. Beginning in the year 937, battles raged between Scotland and England, the first wars of Scottish Independence began in 1296, the Border Wars in 1388, the Anglo-Scottish Wars in 1460 and the Rough Wooing Wars in 1545. From 1040 to 1745, all the English monarchs, except three, either endured Scottish invasions or made invasions into Scotland.

Not only did the Scottish people endure many wars with England, but they also had to endure great violence among themselves. Noblemen took the law into their own hands. Lairds, who were landholders and members of the gentry but not noblemen, did the same. Noblemen feuded with

King Edward III of England Invades Scotland. Painting from Froissart's Chronicles, *1322–1331, by Jean Froissart. Courtesy of Wikimedia Commons.*

other noblemen and lairds with other lairds. The Scottish farmers made up their armies. The farmers were all soldiers and considered fighting as a way of life. Feudalism was the rule, and little organized justice existed. Cattle and sheep were stolen from farmers on a regular basis. The farmers went to the feudal overlords to ask for help in regaining the stolen stock. Naturally, when the overlord's army of farmers found the stolen herd, they always took more than was originally stolen, perpetuating the vicious cycle of violence. The lords considered an injury to any person or thing, even indirectly connected to him, a personal insult that had to be avenged. His main reason for existence was to aid those in his protection. Without him, the farmers were completely vulnerable. But the lords were without principle, and they were tyrants. Officials of the king, who tried to maintain order, were treated badly. When they tried to deliver summons, the papers were torn to bits in their presence. They were often beaten and sometimes killed. The lowlands of Scotland were a place of constant violence. Because there was so much violence, family relationships were critical to survival. Clans were extremely important, much more important than loyalty to the monarchy. An officer who attempted to keep the peace among lowlanders wrote in 1611, "They are void of conscience, the fear of God; and of all honesty, and so linked in a friendship by marriage, and all or most of them of one flesh, ending to make their pain by stealing, that of a hundred felonies scarcely one shall be proved."

The lowlanders settled their differences by violence and blood money, which bought protection from families with great power.

The Scots, primarily lowlanders, began to migrate to Ireland in 1606 and continued to do so into the early 1700s. The reasons for the migration were basically economic. A new tenant agreement had been introduced in Scotland that put tremendous economic pressure on the tenant farmers and caused them to lose possession of their farms. Many farmers were forced to become laborers or subtenants. Some became beggars. King James I saw this as an opportunity. For the prior century, there had been almost constant uprisings in Catholic Ireland against English rule, which caused great expense to the English treasury. King James I theorized that if he brought in Scottish Protestants, he could pacify and civilize the Irish. He ordered the seizure of farmlands in Ulster from rebel Irish chieftains and other native landowners and redistributed the land to wealthy men from England and Scotland. All the tenants and workers for the farms had to be from Scotland and England, none from Ireland. There were also religious reasons for the migration from Scotland to Ireland. King James I had attempted to have the Presbyterian Book

King James I of England. *Painting by Daniel Mytens, 1621, National Portrait Gallery, London. Courtesy of Wikimedia Commons.*

of Common Order written more in keeping with the Anglican Book of Common Prayer. Scots across the country refused to make the changes. When King Charles I took the throne in 1625, he ordered that the Presbyterian order of service be replaced by the Anglican high church form of worship. The Scots believed he was trying to revive Catholicism in Scotland. Migration to Ireland continued to grow. It is estimated that by the end of the seventeenth century, 200,000 lowland Scots had migrated to Ulster. The Scots, however, didn't escape fighting by going to Ireland. The Scotch-Irish had to withstand numerous uprisings of Irish trying to retake their Ulster lands. Then, in 1689, King James II, using papal forces, attempted to wipe out the Protestants in Ulster. The Scotch-Irish prevailed in all these conflicts. The Scots knew how to fight for what they believed was theirs. Sir Walter Scott best summed up the warring nature of the people of Scotland when he wrote, "I am a Scotsman, therefore I had to fight my way into the world."

The reasons for leaving Ireland and coming to America were also primarily economic. In surveys taken in the 1700s, the Scotch-Irish were asked why they migrated from Ireland. Famine and starvation were the answers given most often. Although they met with a lot of disdain from the other cultural groups in America, the immigrants gave little thought to returning because the conditions they had left were so deplorable. One Scotch-Irish immigrant in Pennsylvania in 1767 wrote, "I do not know one that has come here that desires to be in Ireland again." Although most of the Scotch-Irish appeared to look very poor and were considered scum by the other ethnic groups, the majority had been able to pay their own passenger fares on the journey by ship to America. Most of the immigrants were farmers and farm laborers. They weren't landowners but were sometimes tenants and subtenants. In

America, the Scotch-Irish held out the dream of owning their own land. A substantial number were out-of-work weavers from the linen trade and small-time traders. About 25 percent were servants, but the majority of servants were not indentured. There wasn't much demand for servants in America, and the Scotch-Irish servants were considered unmanageable and sometimes violent. A very small percent of the Scotch-Irish immigrants, perhaps 1 to 2 percent, were gentry, who naturally became the leading men in the communities. The Scotch-Irish, including the family of Reverend Alexander Craighead, initially came to America through Boston but soon made Philadelphia their primary port of entry. They began to move farther and farther south because of the low cost of land, and by 1775, North Carolina had the third-highest number of Scotch-Irish, behind only Pennsylvania and Virginia. In that year, the Scotch-Irish population in North Carolina was 35,000 and the total number of Scotch-Irish in America was 220,000, which represented 9.8 percent of the total white population.

The same lack of respect for the authority of the officials of the Scottish king was brought with the Scotch-Irish to America. The Scotch-Irish tended to settle on the frontiers of the colonies, not only because land was cheaper but also because they wanted to be as far away from the authorities as possible. Unlike the other American cultural groups, they had very little formal organization in their local governments. They didn't have town meetings, vestries or commissions, and their courts had little authority. In the backcountry, rich and poor men considered one another, for the most part, as social equals. They dressed alike, mostly in Indian clothes, and addressed one another by their first names. They labored, ate, played and fought Indians together as equals. The Anglican missionary Charles Woodmason couldn't understand way the Scotch-Irish didn't give him the respect he felt he was due. He wrote in his journal about their insolence and impudence, and he stated that they were "the most audacious of any set of mortals I ever met with." Backcountry militiamen often refused to follow orders of officers, unless convinced to do so. The real authority lay with men of influence who held no public office but had earned the respect of the people. They usually were large landowners, merchants, surveyors, millers and speculators. They acted as judges and arbiters of most feuds, bickerings and disagreements, and their rulings were usually accepted by both parties. Sometimes, the men of influence were magistrates, but only if the respect of the settlers had been earned. The authority of the judges usually carried little weight. Often, their rulings were ignored. In South Carolina in 1767, when a number of magistrates attempted to try a group of banditti, the offenders seized the judges and tried them in a mock court. One of the magistrates was punished by being dragged eighty miles behind a horse. A traveler in the backcountry wrote of the Scotch-Irish, "They shun everything which appears to demand of them law and order, and anything that preaches constraint. They hate the name of justice, and yet they are not transgressors…Altogether, natural freedom…is what pleases them."

The Scotch-Irish did have great respect for their own system of justice. That system was built on the concept that a good man seeks to do right, but if he is done wrong, he must punish the offender himself by retaliation and thus restore order and justice. A North Carolina proverb sums it up with the words, "Every man should be sheriff on his own hearth." During the 1760s, vigilante groups formed in the southern Scotch-Irish backcountry. In one instance, a bold group of banditti attempted to steal all the horses of parishioners while they were worshipping in a church. The vigilantes reported that they had "pursued the rogues, broke up their gangs, burnt the dwellings of all their harborers and abetters—whipped 'em and drove the vile, vicious and profligate out of the province, men and women without distinction." The vigilantes subscribed to what was known as "Lynch's Law," which was likely named after Captain William Lynch of Pittsylvania County, Virginia. The law, which became a formal agreement among backcountry neighbors in the county, read: "Whereas, many of the inhabitants of Pittsylvania had sustained great and intolerable losses by a set of lawless men…we will inflict such corporeal punishment on him or them, as to be adequate to the crime committed or the damage sustained."

The actions of the vigilantes were very fast. Offenders were whipped and sometimes slain without much regard for evidence. Feuds were very common between individuals, families, clans and communities. They might occur over stolen property or injuries and even insults and jealousies. Often, feuds went on for years. The famous Hatfield and McCoy feud went on for over twenty years in the 1800s between the two Scotch-Irish families. The Hatfields lived on the Virginia side of the Tug Fork River, and the McCoys lived on the Kentucky side. A McCoy was murdered in 1865, presumedly by a Hatfield, but it was never proven. The Hatfields hated the McCoy clan member because he fought on the Union side in the Civil War. The feud escalated in 1878 when a Hatfield kept a McCoy razorback hog, which had wandered onto his property. During the Hatfield-McCoy feud, more than twenty people were killed and more wounded. It didn't die down until 1888, when a number of participants were hanged by the civil authorities for the killings. William "Devil Anse" Hatfield, the leader of

Hatfield clan. *Photo from* Iowa State Press, *February 11, 1889. Courtesy of Wikimedia Commons.*

his clan, was asked why he had killed so many McCoys, and he answered, "A man has a right to defend his family." By family, he meant the clan. The Scotch-Irish looked at the severity of crimes differently than the other American cultures. Property crimes were considered much worse than crimes of personal violence. This was true in the vigilante system, as well as in the public courts. During the 1700s, a court in Cumberland County, Virginia, made a judgment of death for hog stealing, while giving a one-shilling fine for the rape of an eleven-year-old girl.

The Scotch-Irish raised their boys to be fighters and resist authority. Unlike the New England Puritans, who deliberately attempted to break the will of their children, the Scotch-Irish tried to strengthen the will of their boys. Their main goal was to instill tremendous pride, obstinate independence and fighting courage in the young boys. This produced a society of adults who were quick to rage, lacked respect for authority and demonstrated little self-control. Boys were raised with extreme leniency and tolerance and were taught to defend their honor without thinking and with vicious violence. Parents doted on their sons. One observer of the Scotch-Irish backcountry culture wrote, "Parents often look on it as evidence of spirit and smartness to see their children rudely insulting the quiet and often humble citizens of the country." When a boy put on his first pair of breeches, he was given great freedom around the settler's property and often received a small axe or knife with which to play. The concept of corporeal punishment was frowned upon in theory but in reality was used quite often. Parents were normally indulgent, but they would become frustrated by their sons and their rage would take over. Beatings were not rare and were often aggravated by problems of alcohol. Girls were raised in a completely different manner. Mothers taught their daughters submissiveness, forbearance, sacrifice, fidelity to others and self-denial. The young girls were trained to become obedient wives for their future husbands.

The lack of respect that the Scotch-Irish had for authority in general was shown by the way they treated the Anglican missionary Charles Woodmason. He reported on how they changed the posted dates of his sermons, stole the keys to his church, passed out whiskey bottles to his parishioners about two hours before he preached and provided Woodmason with incorrect directions. His journal read:

> *I had appointed a Congregation to meet me at the Head of Hanging Rock Church—When I arriv'd on Tuesday evening—Found the Houses filled with debauch'd licentious fellows, and Scot Presbyterians who had hir'd these lawless Ruffians to insult me, which they did with Impunity—Telling me, they wanted no D—d Black Gown Sons of Bitches among them...In the Morning the lawless Rabble moved off on seeing the Church people appear, of whom had a large Congregation. But the service was greatly interrupted by a gang of Presbyterians who kept hallooing and whooping without Door like Indians.*

On one occasion, the Scotch-Irish hired a bunch of men to come to Woodmason's church with fifty-seven dogs (he said he counted them) and set the dogs to fighting at the time of the service. He also took note of the way the Scotch-Irish fought among themselves, writing, "The perverse persecuting spirit of the Presbyterians displays itself much more here than in Scotland...the sects are eternally jarring among themselves." Woodmason tried to solve his problems with the Scotch-Irish by appealing to local officials, but with no success. He wrote, "As all magistrates are Presbyterians, I could not get a warrant...if I got warrants, as the constables are Presbyterians likewise I could not get them served." He wrote that they were "insolent" and "impudent" and were "the most audacious of any set of mortals I ever met with." Woodmason blamed all the actions of the Scotch-Irish people on the Presbyterian preachers and wrote in his journal, "These roving [Presbyterian] Teachers stir up the Minds of the People against the Establish'd Church, and her Ministers…I find them a Sett of Rhapsodists—Enthusiasts—Bigots—Pedantic, illiterate, impudent Hypocrites—Straining at Gnats, and swallowing Camels, and making Religion a Cloak for Covetousness, Detraction, Guile, Impostures and their particular Fabric of Things."

It was true that Presbyterian ministers, and Reverend Alexander Craighead in particular, had a tremendous influence on their parishioners, but the culture of the Scotch-Irish had been passed down from generation to generation over centuries.

The violence of the Scotch-Irish was also reflected in the names they chose for their North Carolina towns, such as Bloody Rock, Cutthroat Gap, Gallows Branch, Bloodrun Creek, Breakneck Ridge, Hanging Rock, Killquick, Whipping Creek and Skull Camp Mountain. The sports that they chose to play as children and adults were also violent. Boys played games of wrestling and fighting. A game that started on the borderlands in Scotland and was brought to America was "Scots and English," in which two teams of boys put their hats and coats behind them and each team attempted to get the other team's clothes without getting caught, while they made loud war shouts. The respect that the Scotch-Irish had for warriors was shown in the names they chose for their sons. They used the last name of warrior Robert Bruce as a first name because, as king of Scotland, he led the country to independence from England. They did the same with warrior Sir William Wallace, a Scottish landowner who also led Scotland to independence. Another name used was Alexander, a king of Scotland who was such a fighter that he was known as "The Fierce." The name David was taken from the Bible because he slew Goliath with just a sling and a stone and then used Goliath's own sword to behead him. As grown men, the Scotch-Irish would engage in two types of wrestling (wrassling) matches. One was regulated and controlled, and the other was called "rough and tumble," with a

Sir William Wallace. Illustration for book by William Blake, circa 1819. *Courtesy of Wikimedia Commons.*

no-holds-barred approach that went on until one man gave up. Some of these fights ended with a man blinded from a gouging of his eyes or the loss of a portion of an ear or nose from biting.

The Scotch-Irish were a rough, tenacious people. This was shown in their housing. The typical homes of the Scotch-Irish were log cabins, vastly different from the other houses in the colonies. In New England, houses were made of wood, hardwoods when they were abundant and softwoods thereafter. The houses of the English settlers in Virginia were very handsome, primarily made of brick, and included several outbuildings. The homes of the Quakers in Pennsylvania were mostly made of fieldstone. The Scotch-Irish cabin concept had been utilized by the settlers both in the Scottish lowlands and in Ireland and contained one open room. The walls were rectangular, and the floors were hard-packed dirt. The roofs were made of either bark or split boards. There were a few simple openings for windows, small holes for firing rifles and a door in the front and back for fast exits from Indians and other intruders. The buildings were made of the cheapest materials available. In Scotland, that was stone and dirt; in Ireland, the cabins were made of turf and mud; and in America, since the Scotch-Irish settled on the frontiers of the colonies, they were built with logs and clay. Typically, the log cabins were about sixteen to seventeen feet long, and if the owners needed more space, they would build two cabins side by side with an open covered breezeway. Some of their log cabins used a fire pit with a hole

Log cabin from the 1700s. *Photo by author.*

in the roof to let the smoke escape, while others contained an open fireplace, made of stones and clay, on a side wall. Iron pots were hung over the fire and used for cooking. The dim lighting came from the fireplace, candles and oil lamps. The furniture was homemade, with tables of hewn planks, benches and some chests. Beds were typically rough frames with straw mattresses. Not only were the houses crude and impermanent, but the outbuildings, such as barns, were as well. They were often made of saplings and boughs. Cattle was corralled into simple cowpens, which were moved around the farm to fertilize the land. When the cattle had produced enough dung in one area, the cowpens would be easily moved to an area needing fertilization.

Among the other American cultures, the Scotch-Irish were thought of as a crude, unsophisticated class of people. They called themselves "rednecks" and were called that name by others, having brought the term with them from Scotland. In the 1640s, the king of England, Charles I, tried to impose the Anglican system of church government with its bishops on Scotland. The Presbyterian Covenanters completely rejected the rule of bishops and often signed manifestos to that effect using their own blood. They also wore red cloths around their necks to signify their position against bishops. In America, the term rednecks became broadened to mean a derogatory name for poor, uneducated white farmers, especially in the southern states.

The settlers lived off the crops they grew; the abundant forest game, such as deer, bear, elk and buffalo; and the fish they caught in the rivers and creeks. The women ground the corn into meal from which they prepared bread and cakes. The corn was also fermented to make whiskey, which the Scotch-Irish had long consumed in Scotland and Ireland. In addition, the corn whiskey was used as cash for the purchase of needed supplies, including ammunition and tools. The settlers found that apple, pear, peach and plum trees grew very well on the southern frontier and provided additional food. The fruit was also fermented to make brandy, which quickly became the second choice to whiskey. Even with the great variety of food available to them, the backcountry settlers tended to eat very simple suppers, consisting of a wooden bowl of milk and mush, seasoned with a little bit of bear oil. The mush was usually cornmeal and sometimes oatmeal, which was cooked by boiling and called "grits." Another common dish was clabber, which was sour milk, curds and whey. They also ate a lot of hearthbread, griddle cakes and pancakes. The ingredients changed, but typically they were all made of unleavened dough and baked on a flat bakestone in an open hearth. The same foods had been eaten on the borders of Scotland and brought to America. Visitors to the backcountry were shocked by the

King Charles I of England. *Painting by Anthony Van Dyck, 1636, Royal Collection, Windsor Castle, England. Courtesy of Wikimedia Commons.*

food of the Scotch-Irish. Other American cultures fed this kind of food to their animals. The Anglican minister Charles Woodmason wrote, "The people are all from Ireland, and live wholly on butter, milk, clabber and what in England is given to hogs." In general, the way that the Scotch-Irish cooked was shocking to travelers to the backcountry. The settlers didn't worry about cleaning their cooking pots. One visitor was amazed when a wife washed her feet in the pot for cooking. It was considered unlucky to wash out a milk churn. A common saying was, "The mair dirt the less hurt." When it came time to retire to bed, another visitor was very surprised when the hostess gave him a tablecloth for a sheet.

The way in which the Scotch-Irish settlers divided the roles between men and women differed greatly from New England Puritans, Pennsylvania Quakers and Virginia Anglicans. The men were the warriors, and the women were the workers, the roles brought with them from the lowlands of Scotland. The men and women worked together on the farms throughout the whole growing season. Females took care of the livestock and slaughtered the animals. One visitor was greatly surprised when a Scotch-Irish wife slaughtered a bull with an axe, removed her bloody apron, fixed her hair and invited the visitor in for tea. Women performed tasks of tree clearing for farmland and plowed the fields. There were sharp distinctions between men and women emphasizing their masculinity and femininity by the way they acted, talked and dressed and in their decorum and status. There was also little equality between the sexes. Scotch-Irish backcountry families were dominated by the men, much more so than in the other American cultures. The husband was expected to run the household. The wife was to do as she was told and to do it happily and without objection. Husbands would often physically attack their wives, which seldom occurred in other English-speaking American cultures.

Another unusual custom of the Scotch-Irish backcountry was the abduction of the bride. There were two types of abductions, one in which the bride was a willing participant, but the family hadn't approved, and the other in which the bride was taken by force. Neither approach was condemned by the community. This custom was also used in the Old Country, and abductions were frequent in the lowlands of Scotland and in Ulster. There they were regulated by a required payment of a "body price" and "honor price." Abductions of both types continued in America into the late eighteenth century. Court petitions in North Carolina in the 1700s recorded that "their wives and daughters were carried captives" by opposing clans. One famous person who abducted his bride was Andrew Jackson. The future president

Andrew Jackson. *Painting by Thomas Sully, 1824, U.S. Senate Building, Washington, D.C. Courtesy of Wikimedia Commons.*

of the United States, a Scotch-Irishman named Andrew Jackson, grew up in Mecklenburg County. He was born in Waxham, North Carolina, twelve miles south of present-day Charlotte, in 1767, just a year after Reverend Craighead died. In 1788, he met Rachel Robards while he was boarding at her mother's house in Nashville, Tennessee. She was in an unhappy marriage to Lewis Robards, and quarrels between Rachel and Lewis led Jackson to threaten Robards that he would "cut his ears out of his head." Jackson was arrested, but before the trial, he chased Robards with a knife and Robards disappeared. Because there was no plaintiff, the case was dismissed. Jackson abducted the willing Rachel, saying she had been abandoned, and they were married. It was found that she wasn't legally divorced, and they had to get married a second time when her divorce became official. This time they were married by Alexander Craighead's son Reverend Thomas Craighead, a Presbyterian preacher in Nashville. Jackson's abduction of Rachel became a campaign issue in other areas of the country when he ran for president, but the Scotch-Irish population saw no problem with his approach to marriage.

The fiery preaching of Reverend Alexander Craighead with his call for freedom from England and resistance to colonial authorities had a receptive audience among his fighting, defiant Scotch-Irish parishioners in a setting far removed from the royal coastal governor and his council. The dynamics were in place for the revolutionary acts that followed.

Chapter 3

THE WAR OF SUGAR CREEK

Reverend Alexander Craighead's constant preaching about the need for resistance to colonial authorities led to confrontations with the sheriff in Mecklenburg County in 1762. It involved the quitrents and taxes on land granted to a London merchant, Henry McCulloch, and his associates by the king of England, George III, in 1737. The king awarded 1,200,000 acres of land in the foothills of North Carolina for quitrents of four shillings per 100 acres on the condition that they would settle six thousand people on their lands. In 1744, the surveyor-general of North Carolina divided the land into twelve tracts of 100,000 acres each, with Tract Number Three, which was within the area that became Mecklenburg County, assigned to McCulloch's associate John Selwyn. McCulloch and his associates were given until March 14, 1756, to meet the condition of the number of settlers, but because of the Cherokee War, that date was extended until March 25, 1760. Because they weren't going to meet the new date, they were allowed to reduce the number of settlers to one for each 200 acres. The first settlers weren't bothered by the landowners' agents, but in 1760, the colonial government began to actively seek the collection of land taxes. Governor Arthur Dobbs of North Carolina, who was one the associate landowners, attempted to get the boundary dispute between North and South Carolina resolved because the settlers were using it to avoid paying taxes. The settlers in south Mecklenburg County believed their land was in South Carolina and that colony's government had promised them they wouldn't have to pay land taxes. They also believed that George Augustus Selwyn, who was given the royal grant of land in Mecklenburg County, had not met the conditions of the 1737 land purchase. The settlers also believed that, because they had made heavy investments in the land, they should own the land by default. Some of the settlers had gotten county titles soon after they arrived, but according to the deeds recorded in the Mecklenburg County Courthouse, most of them didn't until the beginning of 1767, and some didn't secure a clear title until many years later. Governor Dobbs petitioned King George III, writing:

> *We further beg leave most humbly to represent to your Majesty in Council excepting those Lawless people who are settled upon Sugar and Reedy Creeks and have been before mentioned as the cause of these disturbances it would be far most easy and agreeable to all the North East side of the present Boundary Line to remain annexed to this Government as by our Constitution they can have Justice administrated at their doors.*

George Augustus Selwyn, who had inherited the Tract Number Three land from his father, asked Henry Eustace McCulloch, son of Henry McCulloch, to act as his agent to collect taxes from the settlers on his property. Because H.E. McCulloch knew the character of the settlers in that area, he begged off from that responsibility, but his father demanded it of him, and he agreed to be Selwyn's agent. He warned Governor Dobbs on October 8, 1762:

> *And these Informants further say, that though the Settlers on Sugar and Reedy Creeks live in the part of…this province, no officer or Justice from either Province dare meddle with them, their number rendering them formidable, there being near 150 families settled together, in General, and indeed almost all together people of desperate fortune, and without any property or possession but that of the said patentees Land which they hold by force; who unite together to repel what they call an injury offered any one of them…Sometime ago upon Complaint being made to the County Court of Anson by Townsend Robertson the then High Sheriff of that County, that he had been abused and Insulted by some of these settlers on Sugar and Reedy Creeks, in the Execution of the Duty of his office Orders were given to him to raise the posse comitatus to apprehend them of which they having notice collected themselves together and upon his and his Associates endeavoring to execute such orders and their beginning to behave in a riotous manner the said Sheriff in the King's Name commanded the peace upon*

Left: Governor Arthur Dobbs of North Carolina. *Painting by William Hoare, 1755, Castle Dobbs, Carrickergus, Northern Ireland.*

Below: George Augustus Selwyn (standing). *Painting by Henry Graves, 1865, National Portrait Gallery, London. Courtesy of Wikimedia Commons.*

> *which they damned the King and his peace, and beat and wounded several of those whom the Sheriff had called to his Assistance.*

McCulloch is referring to an incident that occurred earlier that year, in which settlers in the Sugar Creek area, very likely almost all members of Reverend Craighead's Sugaw Creek church, verbally abused and beat men in the sheriff's posse, who were attempting to arrest the settlers because they had earlier abused and insulted the sheriff in his attempts to collect quitrents.

In February 1765, Henry Eustace McCulloch arrived in Mecklenburg County with his party for the purpose of surveying the land near Sugar Creek and to collect quitrents due to Selwyn. McCulloch was acting as Selwyn's agent for Tract Number Three in Mecklenburg County. It was one of twelve tracts in the backcountry granted to Selwyn by King George II of England. McCulloch was there as a representative of Governor Dobbs, who had gained permission from King Charles III of England to survey the land to determine the proper North and South Carolina boundary line. The settlers in the Sugar Creek area had been able to prevent Governor Dobbs from getting them ejected from their property by frightening court officials, who were too scared to serve legal papers in the area. South Carolina also afforded protection to the settlers because of the confusion over the boundary line between the two colonies. A year earlier, in March 1764, McCulloch had met with Thomas Polk, who had been appointed justice of the peace for the new Mecklenburg County, and three other representatives of the settlers to discuss prices for the land.

Thomas Polk was one of the earliest settlers in the area, and the Polk family had grown into the largest clan in Mecklenburg County during the 1700s. Although he was Scotch-Irish, he wasn't a member of any of Reverend Craighead's churches, but he had several connections to people who were members. Thomas Polk had married Susannah Spratt, daughter of Thomas Spratt, who was the first settler between the Yadkin River and the Catawba River. Spratt's eldest daughter, Anne, was the first white child born in what became Mecklenburg County. The Spratt family were all members of the Steele Creek church. A son of Thomas Polk and Susannah, William Polk, and his three sons all became devout Presbyterian Church attendees. Thomas Polk's daughter Margaret married Dr. Ephraim Brevard, who was an elder of the Hopewell church. It is likely that Thomas Polk was a deist and rejected dogmatic Presbyterian theology. It was well known that his younger brother Ezekiel Polk, whom Thomas raised after the early death of their parents, was a deist. Ezekiel's son Samuel was another known deist,

Thomas Polk. *Ink drawing by Jean Plumer.*

as was Samuel's son James K. Polk, the eleventh president of the United States. Although Thomas Polk might not have attended church, he was well aware of Reverend Craighead's preachings about independence and resistance to colonial authorities.

McCulloch, Thomas Polk and the three other representatives had agreed that the settlers would pay within a certain price range in pounds for each one hundred acres of land based on the condition of the property, but when McCulloch returned in March 1765, the settlers had decided that they didn't have to buy from Selwyn because he didn't have clear title to the land. Governor Arthur Dobbs had died in March, and the new governor, William Tryon, had ordered that all surveying cease until the General Assembly could take up the matter of whether the royal land grantees had met the terms of the land grants and were entitled to any quitrents. In spite of the governor's order, McCulloch decided to proceed with the illegal surveying of land. When members of McCulloch's party were in the process of surveying in the Sugar Creek area, they were met by armed men in opposition to his actions. Trying to defuse the situation, McCulloch asked the settlers to meet him the next day at the home of Abraham Alexander of Sugar Creek. When he arrived at the house, he was met by 150 armed men led by Thomas Polk. It is likely that the great majority of these men were parishioners of Reverend Craighead. During the meeting, McCulloch attempted to convince the farmers that their group pact was illegal, but that seemed to have little impact on the men. The settlers agreed among themselves on a new price, which was about 30 percent less than the price that had been agreed to a year earlier by their representatives. McCulloch flatly rejected the offer, and then Thomas Polk warned McCulloch that "the best usage he could expect to meet with would be to be tied Neck and heels and be carried on the Yadkin, and that he might think himself happy, if he got off so." McCulloch realized that Polk was no longer trying to negotiate a price for the settlers but had become their rebellious leader. Polk then declared that "neither he nor the People would ever suffer any Sheriff or other official to serve any precepts upon them on Mr. Selwyn's behalf; or permit [McCulloch] to run out any of the land, not even for Persons who were desirous to agree to the Terms & purchase from Mr. Selwyn." After the meeting, McCulloch and his party attempted to survey a plantation and were prevented from doing so by the settlers. The farmers asked McCulloch whether he thought he "would have as many men attend him to his Grave or not." The settlers took his surveyor's chain from him and broke it, and Thomas Polk removed McCulloch's compass from its stand. Later, on May 7, 1765, McCulloch surveyors were attempting to survey another plantation. They were met by a group of 12 farmers with their faces blackened with soot and led by Thomas Polk. The group attacked the surveyors, including Abraham Alexander, who was "striped from the nape of his neck to the waistband of his Breeches," and "Jimmy Alexander very near had daylight let in his skull." John Frohock and James Norris were also beaten. McCulloch wrote to his friend Edmund Fanning that he felt he would have been killed had he been there. Soon after that, he beat a hasty retreat to New Bern. Later, McCulloch referred to the incident as "the war of Sugar Creek," and the term stuck.

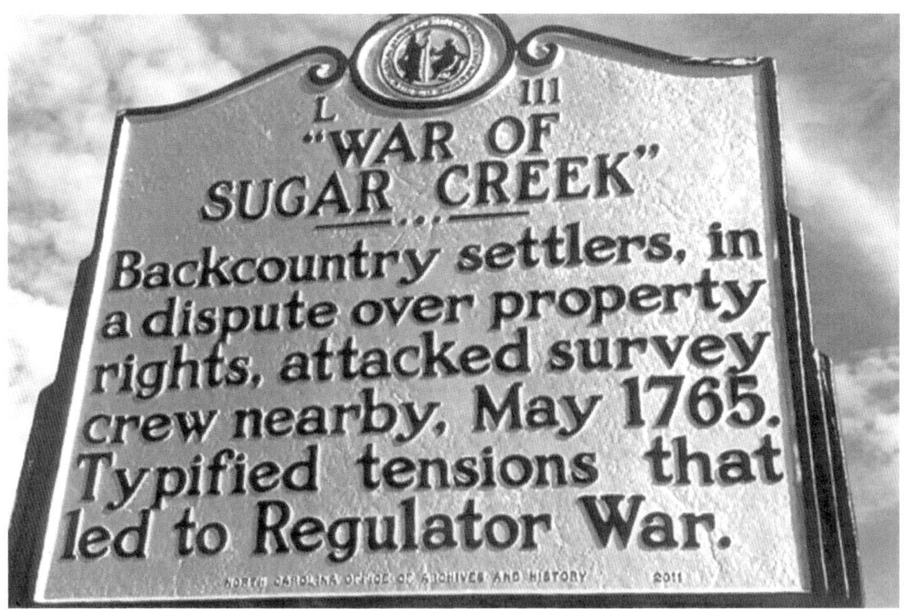

War of Sugar Creek marker. *Photo by Charles Heywood.*

Replica of Mecklenburg County's first courthouse. *Courtesy of Robinson-Spangler Carolina Room, Charlotte Mecklenburg Library.*

Later in 1765, Governor William Tryon attempted to placate the backcountry settlers concerning the land disputes by appointing a commission of two men to examine the royal grants. He named Thomas Polk and Abraham Alexander, who were on opposite sides in the War of Sugar Creek, as the two commissioners. Abraham Alexander, who was an elder at the Sugaw Creek church, was born in Maryland in 1717 and was one of the early settlers in the area that became Mecklenburg County, building a home near the Catawba River. The commission found that the claims of McCulloch and Selwyn were invalid because they had not met the conditions of the original land purchase from the Crown in terms of the number of settlers they had attracted. Governor Tryon ordered that the proprietorships of McCulloch and Selwyn were null and void, and they were required to sell their land to the settlers or to the colonial government. Lord Augustus Selwyn sold 360 acres of land to Abraham Alexander, Thomas Polk and John Frohock for ninety pounds to develop the future town of Charlotte.

H.E. McCulloch was ruthless in his business dealings. When some of the settlers later began to pay him for the land at a price negotiated between the two prices previously discussed, he offered mortgages for those who couldn't borrow the money on credit, which was difficult to procure. The mortgage interest rates were exorbitant, and when the farmers missed a payment, McCulloch sued to get the settler ejected off the property. He then sold the land at a higher rate because of the improvements that had been made by the farmers. The American Revolution resulted in his property being confiscated, and he lost thousands of pounds of his investments. He died years later in an asylum. The settlers of Mecklenburg County generally felt he got what he deserved.

Mecklenburg settlers in 1766, led by Thomas Polk, erected a courthouse on the property at the intersection of the Great Philadelphia Wagon Trail and another major Indian trail at their own expense. The intersection eventually became the corner of Trade and Tyron Streets. They did so because they wanted Charlotte to be named the county seat of Mecklenburg. A bill was introduced in the North Carolina Assembly to incorporate Charlotte and to allow one hundred acres of the town to be laid out in a gridiron of streets with half-acre lots. The annual rent of each lot was to be one shilling, paid to the town treasurer, and a dwelling had to be built on the lot within three years on penalty of forfeiture. The bill was finally passed in November 1768, and by that time, eighty lots had already been reserved, and some already had log cabin homes built on them. Charlotte wasn't made the permanent county seat and given a regular town government until about eight years later when a bill introduced by Thomas Polk in the North Carolina Assembly was finally passed in March 1774.

Chapter 4

REVEREND ALEXANDER CRAIGHEAD'S DEATH

Reverend Craighead's family had grown up during the time he lived in Mecklenburg County, and many had married. Of the eight children of Alexander and Agnes, three daughters married ministers and one son became a minister. There were also several ministers among their grandchildren and great-grandchildren. The eldest daughter, Margaret, married James Carruth in 1764, and they had five children. The second daughter, Mary, married Samuel Dunlap and had three sons, one of whom became a minister in Columbia, South Carolina, and another son's boy became a minister in Pennsylvania. The third daughter, Agnes Nancy, married Reverend William Richardson in 1759 but had no children. The fourth daughter, Rachel, married Reverend David Caldwell in 1766 and had ten children, two of whom became ministers. Reverend David Caldwell became minister of two Presbyterian churches in Alamance and Buffalo in an area that is now Greensboro, North Carolina, and their son Reverend Samuel Craighead Caldwell became minister of the Sugaw Creek church in 1791. Reverend Alexander Craighead's great-grandson, Reverend John Madison McKnitt Caldwell, also became the minister of the Sugaw Creek church in 1837 and remained there until 1845. That the Sugaw Creek church called so many of Reverend Craighead's descendants to be preachers is indicative of how much the congregation respected him. Another son of David and Rachel, Reverend Alexander Caldwell, became pastor of the Rocky River church in 1793. The fifth daughter of Alexander, Jane, married Patrick Calhoun in 1766 but died miscarrying twins in 1767. Patrick and Jane had lived near each other in Virginia. Patrick Calhoun later married Martha Caldwell, and they had a son named John Caldwell Calhoun, who served numerous terms in the United States House and Senate and became vice president under John Quincy Adams and Andrew Jackson. The sixth daughter, Elizabeth, married Alexander Crawford about 1767 and had eight children. The eldest son, Robert, married Hannah Clark and became one of the first settlers in Knoxville, Tennessee. He was an officer in the Revolutionary War and served with distinction under Brigadier General Thomas Sumter. The youngest son, Thomas, married Elizabeth Brown, who was the daughter of Reverend John Brown, a minister in the Hanover Presbytery with Reverend Alexander Craighead. Thomas and Elizabeth had eight children, and Thomas became a minister in Nashville, Tennessee, as well as president of Davidson Academy, which eventually became the University of Nashville.

Reverend William Richardson, who married Reverend Craighead's third daughter, Agnes Nancy, was a pastor of a Presbyterian church in the Waxham, North Carolina, not far from Charlotte. His parishioners, like so many other Presbyterians, received the disdain of Anglican missionary Charles Woodmason, who wrote in 1767:

> *This is a very fruitful Spot, thro' which the dividing line between North and South Carolina runs—The heads of the P.D. River, Lynch's Creek, and many other Creeks take their Rise in this quarter—so that a finer Body of Land is no where to be seen—But it is occupied by a Sett of the most lowest vilest Crew breathing—Scotch-Irish Presbyterians from North Ireland—They have built a Meeting House and Have a Pastor, a Scots Man among them—The Rev. William Richardson—a good Sort of Man—He once was of the Church of England, and solicited for Orders, but was refus'd—whereon he went to Pennsylvania, and got ordained by the Presbytery there, who allowed him a Stipend to preach to these people, who in his Brest he heartily condemns—They will not suffer him to use the Lords Prayer. He wants to introduce Watts Psalms in place of the barbarous Scotch version—but they will not admit it. His congregation is very large—This tract of Land being most surprisingly thick settled beyond any Spot in England of its extent—Seldom less than 9, 10, 1200 People assemble of a Sunday—They never heard an Episcopal Minister or the Common Prayer, and were very curious—The Church people among them are thinly scatter'd but they had a numerous progeny for Baptism—rather chusing* [sic] *they should grow up to Maturity without Baptism that they should receive it by the hands of Sectaries* [dissenters from the Church of England].

Woodmason also complained that although Reverend Richardson had invited him to preach at his church in Waxham, the elders of the church had not allowed it.

The fourth daughter of Reverend Craighead, Rachel, married Reverend David Caldwell when she was twenty-four and he was forty-one. Although of vastly different ages, the couple was very compatible. David had seen Rachel when she was about four years old and, as a young man of twenty-one, had attended her father's church meetings at the Middle Octorara Church in Pennsylvania. David and Rachel both believed, along with her father, that the Select could avoid damnation by working toward character perfection with God's grace. They were both born-again Christians, and they believed that the message of salvation must be evangelized to all they met. Rachel was convinced that David would treat her as an equal in his churches in Alamance and Buffalo and in the academy he planned to start. Reverend Caldwell was educated at Reverend William Tennent's Log College and at the College of New Jersey, which became Princeton University. Caldwell Academy, which Reverend Caldwell began in 1767, became the most well known and longest lasting of any of the thirty-three Presbyterian log colleges that were established before the Revolutionary War. At the time the academy closed, almost all the Presbyterian ministers in the South were either graduates of or had taught at the college, about 135 ministers in all. Five governors, fifty U.S. senators and congressmen and numerous doctors attended Caldwell Academy. Rachel got to know all the students at the academy, was extremely kind to them and instructed them in every way possible on their salvation. It was said that "David Caldwell made them scholars, but Mrs. Caldwell made them preachers." The academy stayed open until 1824, and Reverend Caldwell taught about fifty students each year until 1816, when he was ninety-one. David Caldwell also became the community's doctor. A visiting physician had willed his medical books to Reverend Caldwell, and Caldwell studied the books thoroughly. He served the populace of the surrounding area because there was no other doctor in the vicinity. He also purchased as many other medical books as he could find and used a doctor friend, Benjamin Rush, as a consultant for difficult cases. Caldwell received a doctor of medicine degree in 1810 at the age of eighty-five.

The idea of independence from England and the right of settlers to protest their treatment from the government was supported by Reverend Caldwell, but he went about it in a different way from his fiery father-in-law, Reverend Craighead. He taught a calm, calculated and moderate approach to the problems. Most of his parishioners joined the Regulation Movement, protesting colonial government regulations, and Reverend Caldwell did everything he could to ensure their safety. Sometime in early 1776, Reverend Caldwell began to openly preach for independence from England, and in one of his sermons, he stated, "We have therefore come to that trying period in our history in which it is manifest that the Americans must either stoop under the load of the vilest slavery, or resist their imperious and haughty oppressors…our foes are powerful and determined on conquest; but our cause is good; and in the strength of the Lord, who is mightier than all, we shall prevail."

Reverend Caldwell is credited with writing section 32 of the North Carolina State Constitution in 1776, which stated, "That no person who shall deny the being of God, or the truth of the Protestant religion, or the divine authority either of the Old or New Testament, or who shall hold religious principles incompatible with the freedom and safety of the State, shall be capable of holding any office or place of trust or profit, in the civil department within the State."

In 1835, North Carolina amended the constitution to change the word "Protestant" to "Christian." David and Rachel had thirteen children and a marriage that lasted sixty years. David died in 1824 at the age of ninety-nine, and Rachel died the following year at the age of eighty-three.

After a long illness of two years, Reverend Alexander Craighead died in March 1766 at fifty-nine years of age. He "was somewhat disposed to melancholy" during his last years. On April 9, 1765, Reverend Craighead drew up his will, which was recorded in the Office of the Superior Court, Mecklenburg County. The will reads as follows:

> *I Alexander Craighead of Mecklenburg County in No Carolina. Minister of the Gospel being weak in body but of sound mind and perfect mind & memory. Blessed be God for the same calling to mind the uncertainty of my time in this transitory world & that it is appointed for all men once to die; Do make & ordain this my last Will & Testament in manner & form following that is to say I recommend my Soul & Body to God that gave it—As to what world goods that God bestowed upon me I dispose of as follows: Primis. I order that my Just debts & funeral expenses be paid & discharged by my Executors hereafter named.*
>
> *Item. I order it is my will that my beloved wife Jane Craighead shall enjoy & possess the benefit of my plantation where I now live upon longcreek & the whole of it thereof and likewise the use & benefit of all*

Right: Reverend Alexander Craighead's grave. *Photo by author.*

Below: Iron fence around Reverend Craighead's grave. *Photo by author.*

the negroes I now possess for the support of my family during the time she bears my name—

Item. I give & bequeath unto my eldest daughter Margaret five pounds Current money to be delivered five years after my decease—

Item. I give & bequeath unto my daughter Agnes five pounds of Current money to be delivered five years after my decease—

Item. I give & bequeath unto my daughter Jane Sixty pounds hard money or one negro which my Executors shall see fit or most convenient to give besides Horse Saddle & briddle [sic], *bed & its furniture which is to be delivered as soon as convenient after her marriage.*

Item. I give & bequeath the same to each of my other daughters Rachel, Mary & Elizabeth to be delivered agreeable to the same manner as above to my daughter Jane. Item. I give & bequeath to my sons Robert & Thomas all and singular books except Bibles & some other common books that is used in the family.

Item. I order & it is my Will that my land in Augusta County Virginia containing by estimation 310 & my land on fishing creek in county containing by Estimation 500 be sold as soon as opportunity will permit. Item. I order & it is my will that my two sons Robert & Thomas shall be kept at learning till they attain to what learning that can be had in these parts—

Item. I order and it is my will that not withstanding of what is said above concerning lands & negroes that it is not to be understood but that my Executors if they see it necessary for the discharging the above particulars they are hereby impowered [sic] *to sell & make Sufficient titles to the purchase of any part thereof.*

Item. I order & it is my will that my Executors is fully impowered [sic] *to make sufficient Titles or conveyances to the above mentioned two Tracts of land in Virginia & fishing creek—*

Item. I order & it is my will that if my beloved wife shall change her name that shall have her dower or third as the Law directs but if she continues in my name during her natural life she is fully to enjoy what I order above. At her decease what remains of Land & negroes or whatever else shall be Equally among my children.

Item. I nominate and appoint my said wife Jane Craighead & John Davis of this county to be my Executors of this my last Will and Testament and lastly I disannul [sic] *& make void all former Wills & Testaments by me made whether in word or writing, & declare this only to be my last Will & Testament / In witness whereof I have hereto set my hand & Seal this ninth day of April one Thousand seven hundred & sixty five—Signed Sealed Pronounced & Declared by the said Alexander Craighead to be his last Will & Testament in the presence of—*

Alexander Craighead

Nathan Orr

Mildredge Orr

William Orr

Reverend Alexander Craighead was buried in the first cemetery of the Sugaw Creek church, which is located about one half mile west of the present brick church through the woods on W. Craighead Road. The grave is surrounded by an iron fence about six feet by ten feet and has a granite headstone, which reads: "Rev. Alex Craighead, Died March 1766, Monument at Cemetery in Charlotte, N.C." The monument referred to on the gravestone is located in the Elmwood Cemetery near downtown Charlotte on West Sixth Street. It is about twenty feet tall and is inscribed on one side with Reverend Craighead's name and the fact that he was pastor of the Rocky River and Sugaw Creek churches from 1758 to 1766. On another side, it states, "Advocate of American Independence from 1743," and on a third side, "Inspirer of Mecklenburg Declaration." Two poles were used to carry Reverend Craighead's coffin to the graveyard and were pushed into the ground to mark his grave. Tradition has it that the poles took root and grew into two large sassafras trees, which finally fell about 125 years after his death. People came from great distances to get pieces of the trees for souvenirs, and one piece was used to make the top of the present pulpit in the Sugaw Creek Presbyterian Church. Another piece was used to make a small wooden cup, which is on display in the church, and another piece was fashioned into a gavel, which the Synod of North Carolina used during meetings for several years.

Reverend Alexander Craighead Monument. *Photo by author.*

Reverend Alexander Craighead was no longer with the parishioners of his seven churches in Mecklenburg County, but the memory of his fiery preachings on independence from England and resistance to the North Carolina colonial authorities was firmly entrenched in their minds. His convincing rhetoric led those same parishioners to rebellious acts, battles and declarations of independence against the colonial royal government and against England, which preceded by several years similar rebellious acts in northern colonies.

Chapter 5

REBELLION IN MECKLENBURG COUNTY AND THE FOOTHILLS OF NORTH CAROLINA

A movement started in 1766 in the foothills of North Carolina, primarily in the counties of Orange, Rowan, Anson and Mecklenburg, that eventually became known as the Regulator Movement. Some of the Regulators from Mecklenburg County were Robert Caruthers; Benjamin Cochran; Robert Davis; James White Jr.; John White Jr.; William White, son of the widow White; and William White, son of James White, all members of the Rocky River church, as well as Andrew Logan and John Luin. There were likely many more members of the Regulation Movement from Mecklenburg County, but many Regulators remained anonymous because of fears of reprisal. The movement was inspired by the settlers' success in resisting colonial authorities in Mecklenburg County. The group's primary goals were to stop the corrupt behavior of colonial officials, reduce taxation and reverse the colony's unfair laws. Land taxes were collected by local sheriffs, who were supported by the courts. Many of the sheriffs would demand more taxes than the law permitted and keep the extra money for themselves. Sometimes, they would purposely lose tax collection records and extort additional taxes. The governor of North Carolina, William Tryon, supported the system because he feared losing the backing of county officials. The Regulator Movement formed itself into an association in 1767, and announced, "That we will pay no taxes until we are satisfied they are agreeable to law…That we will pay no officer any more fees than the law allows…That we will attend our meetings of conference as often as we conveniently can, and is necessary in order to consult our representatives on the amendment of such laws as may be found grievous or unnecessary."

Governor William Tryon of North Carolina. *Painting by unknown artist, 1767, unknown location. Courtesy of Wikimedia Commons.*

The association published circulars to provide news and information to the individual county groups, and in 1768, the terms "Regulator" and "Regulation" began being used in association publications. Governor Tryon built an expensive home in 1770 in New Bern, which later became known as Tryon Palace. William (the Regulator) Butler is known to have said, "We are determined not to pay the Tax for the next three years, for the edifice for the Governor's house, nor will we pay for it." The Regulators believed that the tax dollars collected were being used wastefully.

The Regulators increased their protests of the corrupt tax practices of local authorities. One of the worst offenders was Sheriff Edmund Fanning in Orange County. Besides charging excessive land taxes, he no longer abided by the common practice of going house to house to collect the taxes. Instead, he insisted that the settlers come to an isolated place, which was often a great distance from the settlers' homes. If the settlers didn't come there to pay their taxes, Fanning raised their tax bills. He became a symbol of political corruption. Herman Husband, an Orange County miller and North Carolina Assembly representative, who was a leader of the Regulators, protested to Governor Tryon, "All we want is to be governed by law, and not the will of officers." Two Regulators walked all the way from Hillsborough to New Bern to show evidence of corruption to the governor. Tryon promised to help, but instead of getting the assembly to act on the corruption problem, he conducted parades of the militia in Charlotte, Hillsboro and Salisbury as a show of military power.

In April 1768, one of the Regulators' mares was seized in Orange County by Sheriff Hawkins because the Regulator could not pay his land taxes. About eighty Regulators assembled at Hillsborough and found Sheriff Hawkins. They made him sit backward on the mare, a very degrading

Tryon Palace. *Courtesy of Wikimedia Commons.*

position, and ride through the town to the jeers of the people on the streets. Two or three bullets were then shot into Sheriff Fanning's house in Hillsborough. The Regulators were trying to get respect for their grievances in a fairly nonviolent way and force the government to correct the problem. Instead, Sheriff Fanning labeled the Regulators as "Rebels, Insurgents…to be shot, hang'd, &c. as mad Dogs." Fanning also had Herman Husband put in jail on May 1, 1768, blaming him for the disorder. Hundreds of citizens marched on Hillsborough to get Husband released. Governor William Tryon called out the local militia, but not nearly as many responded as expected. The governor and Sheriff Fanning confronted the large group of protesters. Tryon told them to disperse and ordered them to pay their taxes but also warned public officials not to charge illegal fees. The militia had no legal right to force the crowd to leave or to attack it because their actions were considered a traditional protest. Sheriff Fanning was forced to release Husband, and the sheriff promised to have the governor address the tax problems. Later, Fanning was tried for charging illegal fees and found guilty but was fined only one penny. Herman Husband, tried for inciting a riot, was found not guilty. Over the next two years, little was done by the government to alleviate the tax problems.

Even though Reverend Craighead had been a revolutionary, other Presbyterian ministers in the western part of the colony became very apprehensive by the actions of the settlers in Mecklenburg and other counties. They saw the Presbyterian inhabitants of Mecklenburg County as leading the movement of rebellion. For that reason, on August 23, 1768, four ministers, specifically Reverend McAden, Reverend James Creswell, Reverend Hugh Pattillo and Reverend David Caldwell, who had married Reverend Craighead's daughter Rachel and preached at churches in Alamance and Buffalo, North Carolina, wrote an open letter to the "Presbyterian Inhabitants of Mecklenburg County" asking them to be true to the king of England and the North Carolina governor. At the same time, the preachers sent a pledge of their allegiance to Governor Tryon.

There were two laws passed by the North Carolina Assembly that caused Presbyterian settlers in Mecklenburg County great hardship. One was the Marriage Act, which ordered that only ministers of the Church of England could perform the rites of matrimony. Civil authorities could perform marriages only if the county had no Anglican minister, which was the case in Mecklenburg County. This meant that Mecklenburg Presbyterians either had to pay fees to the civil authorities or travel great distances to the

Governor William Tryon and the Regulators. *Courtesy of the State Archives of North Carolina.*

nearest Anglican minister, who was in South Carolina, to be married and pay him a fee. Naturally, they wanted to be married by their own minister, and most were, ignoring the law, but they then worried that their children would be considered bastards under the law and inheritance wills might not be honored in the courts. The other law was the Vestry Act, which divided North Carolina into Anglican parishes and required all citizens to pay taxes for the support of the Anglican Church. This placed a hardship on the Scotch-Irish, who supported their own Presbyterian Church and had to support the Anglican Church as well.

In 1769, Hezekiah Alexander and the other magistrates in Mecklenburg County wrote a petition to Governor William Tryon presenting their grievances concerning these two acts. Hezekiah Alexander was born in Maryland in January 1722, and migrated with his family to the area that became Mecklenburg in 1754. He built the first stone house in the area five miles east of present-day downtown Charlotte. The house still stands today as Charlotte's oldest surviving residence. Alexander was part of a large clan in the county, which was primarily based in Catawba County, northwest of Mecklenburg, where even a greater number of Alexanders lived. He was a very active elder in Reverend Craighead's Hopewell church. The document sent to the governor was titled "Petition from the Inhabitants of Mecklenburg County concerning North Carolina church laws," and included the following grievances:

> *We think it is a grievance that we are liable to a burthensome* [sic] *taxation to support Episcopal clergy. We would by no means cast reflection upon our sister church of England; no, let them worship God according to their consciences, without molestation from us. We ask on our part that we may worship God according to our consciences, without molestation from them. We think it as reasonable that those who hold to the Episcopal Church should pay their clergy without our assistance as that we, who hold to the church of Scotland, should pay our clergy without their assistance. We now support two settled Presbyterian ministers in this Parish, we, therefore think it a grievance that the present law makes us liable to be still further burthened* [sic] *with taxes to support an Episcopal clergyman: especially as not one twentieth part of the inhabitants are of that profession. We think that were there an Episcopal clergyman in this Parish, his labours* [sic] *would be useless. We think ourselves highly aggrieved by the exorbitant power of the vestry, to tax us with the enormous sum of ten shillings each taxable; which is more than double the charge of Government: And that for*

Hezekiah Alexander House. *Courtesy of the Robinson-Spangler Carolina Room, Charlotte Mecklenburg Library.*

purposes to which we ought by no means to pay anything by compulsion. We, therefore, think that under the present law, the very being of a vestry in this Parish, will ever be a great grievance. We further think, that were the Counties of Rowan, Mecklenburg and Tryon wholly relieved from the grievances of the marriage act and vestry acts, it would greatly encourage the settlement of the Frontiers, and make them a stronger barrier to the interior parts of the Province against savage enemy. We conceive ourselves highly injured and aggrieved by the marriage act, the preamble whereof scandalizes the Presbyterian clergy, and wrongfully charges them with celebrating the rites of marriage without license or publication of banns. We think it a grievance, that this Act imposes heavy penalties on our clergy, for marrying after publication of banns by them made, in their own religious assemblies, where the parties are best known. We declare that the marriage Act obstructs the natural and inalienable right of marriage and tends to introduce immorality. We declare it subjects many to several inconveniences, one whereof is going into South Carolina to have the ceremony preformed. We pray that the preamble of the same Act may be rescinded; and that

> *our ministers and magistrates may be freed from the penalties thereof, they respectively conforming to the Confession of faith. We pray that we may be relieved from the grievance of the vestry Acts and Acts for supporting the Episcopal clergy. We pray that, to these several grievances, you will in your wisdom and goodness grant that redress, which we ask in this legal and constitutional method.*

The petition also made veiled threats to the governor concerning the strength of the inhabitants of Mecklenburg County and their resolution to have liberty. Near the beginning of the petition, it stated, "We would inform that there are about one thousand freemen of us, who hold to the established church of Scotland able to bear arms, within the county of Mecklenburg." And at the end of the petition, it threatened, "We shall ever be more ready to support that government under which we find the most liberty." With that last statement, Hezekiah Alexander was echoing the teachings of Reverend Alexander Craighead, his preacher for many years at the Hopewell church.

Since the 1768 Regulator demonstration in Hillsborough, little had been done by Governor Tryon and the colonial assembly to correct the problems of political corruption and unfair tax laws. In September 1770, Herman Husband and several other Regulator leaders had trials pending in North Carolina's colonial court in Hillsborough. A large group of angry Regulators, likely including Mecklenburg settlers who had been members of Reverend Craighead's congregations, traveled to Hillsborough and filled up the courthouse, armed with clubs, pitchforks and cow whips. They attempted to get presiding judge Richard Henderson to try the Regulator leaders' cases that day and asked that they be made jury members. The judge and the demonstrators debated the proposal for about thirty minutes, and then the judge continued with the scheduled cases, ignoring the crowd's requests. Frustrated Regulators grabbed a lawyer named Williams outside the courthouse and beat him. They then found Sheriff Edmund Fanning hiding in a shop next to the courthouse and beat him so badly that, according to Judge Henderson, "one of his eyes was almost beaten out." Henderson adjoined the court for the day, fearing that he would be beaten as well. He promised it would be reconvened the next morning but fled town during the night. After the judge left, the Regulators proceeded to vandalize the courthouse, putting human waste on the judge's seat and the body of a dead slave on the lawyer's bar, and broke the windows of several shops in town. The Regulators dragged the beaten body of Fanning out of his house and ran him out of town. They destroyed the furniture in his house, drank all his alcohol, tore down his house board by board, marched his effigy through the town and destroyed a church bell he had donated to the town's Anglican church. The Regulators then burned down the house, barn and stables of Judge Henderson.

On December 5, 1770, the North Carolina Assembly, which included Thomas Polk and Abraham Alexander as the representatives from Mecklenburg County, met in New Bern. They had been given reports that the Regulators were gathering in the backcountry and were preparing to march east and perhaps attack the assembly itself. Governor Tryon spoke at the assembly's first meeting. He mentioned the abuses in the collection of public funds and the complaints against offices and officers, but his main concern was "the Injuries offered to His Majesty's Government at and since the last Hillsborough Superior Court." On December 20, the assembly resolved to expel Herman Husband from its membership, stating that he was a "promotor [*sic*] of the late Riots and seditions in the County of Orange and other parts." They also accused him of lying to a House committee and of insinuating "that in case he should be confined by order of the House he expected…a number of people to release him." The assembly also requested the chief justice to issue a warrant for his arrest for libeling Judge Maurice Moore. The assembly asserted that "it may be of fatal consequence to this Country should he be suffered to rejoin the regulators in the back settlements of this Province." Governor Tryon ordered Herman's arrest on January 31, 1771. Husband was put in jail in New Bern, but the charges of libel were dropped, and he was released.

The assembly did address some of the Regulators' grievances by passing an act regarding sheriffs' appointments and duties, a table of fees for attorneys, militia officers' fees being more strictly regulated, the chief justice being placed on a salary and the legal collection of small debts being simplified. The attorney general had told the governor and his council that the most the Hillsborough disrupters could be charged with was a "riot," which was just a misdemeanor. But Governor Tryon was pushing for a charge of high treason, punishable by death. It seemed unlikely that the Johnston Riot Act, introduced by assemblyman Samuel Johnston, who later became governor of North Carolina, would pass as late as December 21. But then Regulators, having heard of the arrest of Herman Husband, began to assemble at Cross Creek, near present-day Fayetteville, for a march on New Bern to free Husband. This provoked the assembly into passing the Johnston Riot Act on January 10, 1771. The act equated riotous behavior with insurrection. It made it a felony for people to be in unlawful assemblies of ten or more and

Assemblyman Samuel Johnston. *Photo of Johnston's bust by Daderot. Courtesy of Wikimedia Commons.*

not disperse within an hour after getting an order from a judge or sheriff to do so. It also allowed law enforcement to use force without investigation, allowing it to maim or kill the rioters. The law also declared rioters who remained at large for sixty days to be considered outlaws, and it allowed officials to seize and sell the property of outlaws. The law was applied retroactively to the Hillsborough rioters, and it allowed Governor Tryon to raise a militia, using public funds, to execute the law. On February 8, the jury in the Superior Court returned a "no bill" verdict in Herman Husband's libel trial. He was released and met the Regulators gathered at Cross Creek.

In January 1771, the North Carolina Assembly finally reacted to one of the grievances of Hezekiah Alexander and other Presbyterians in the colony and passed an act that allowed regularly called Presbyterian ministers to perform the rite of marriage in their own churches or by license. Surprisingly, the bill was introduced by Sheriff Edmund Fanning, who said that the restrictions on Presbyterian pastors were a great hardship on their congregations, who preferred for the ceremony to be conducted by a minister rather than a justice of the peace. Thomas Polk, who was one of the representatives to the assembly, along with Abraham Alexander at that time, was appointed to a committee to draft the law.

Governor William Tryon was determined to crush the Regulator Movement, and he decided that if he was going to mount a military campaign against it that he needed to move military supplies, including gunpowder and bullets, to Salisbury, where General Hugh Waddell was encamped. The supplies had been shipped from Charleston, South Carolina, and were being stored in Charlotte. In late April 1771, he ordered that the shipment be made. A convoy of several wagons of powder and bullets left Charlotte on May 2, 1771, headed north toward Salisbury, but before it left, the planned movement had been discovered by the Regulators in Mecklenburg County.

Eight young members of the Rocky River church, which was a former church of Reverend Alexander Craighead, volunteered along with one other young man to intercept the wagon train. Their names were Robert Caruthers; Benjamin Cochran; Robert Davis; John Headley; James White; John White; William White, son of James; and William White, son of the widow White. The ninth member of the volunteer group was named James Ashmore. They were led by William Alexander, who was a member of Reverend Craighead's Sugaw Creek church. The men dressed up as Indians and blackened their faces. They caught up with the wagoners camped at Phifer's Hill, three miles west of present-day Concord, on the road from Charlotte to Salisbury. The area was still in north Mecklenburg County at that time. The wagoners had eaten their supper and were sound asleep, when the Mecklenburg Black Boys, as they came to be known, crept up to the ammunition wagons. They unloaded the powder and dumped it in a large pile, along with bullets, blankets, leggings and kettles. Then a powder trail was laid out from the pile. James White fired his pistol into the powder trail, and a large explosion ignited the powder and other materials in the pile and caused great damage to other equipment in the wagons. While they were preparing the pile, one of the wagon drivers, James Caruthers, awoke and recognized one of the Mecklenburg Black Boys as his brother Robert. Speaking in a low voice, James said, "You'll rue this, Bob," and Robert responded with, "Hold your tongue, Jim." Some six years later, both brothers fought together in the Revolutionary War on the side of the Americans. The Mecklenburg Black Boys were able to make their escape without any shots being fired by either the Black Boys or the wagoners. William Alexander became known as "Black Billy" because of the incident. Later in 1771, Governor Tryon made a proclamation with an offer of pardon to the Regulators if they made a pledge of loyalty to the Crown, except to "all those concerned in blowing up General Waddell's

British general Hugh Waddell. *Illustration from* A Colonial Officer and His Times, *1890, by Alfred Moore Waddell. Courtesy of Wikimedia Commons.*

Ammunition." The actions of the Mecklenburg Black Boys was a direct result of the preachings of Reverend Alexander Craighead, who for eight years taught his parishioners independence from England and resistance to colonial authorities. The revolutionary act occurred more than two years before the destruction of British tea by Patriots in the Boston Tea Party on December 6, 1773, and should be recognized as a significant event in the American movement toward independence and equally as important as the Patriots' heroism in Boston's harbor.

Chapter 6

THE FIRST BATTLE OF THE REVOLUTIONARY WAR

On May 4, 1771, Governor Tryon was encamped with his army at Hunter's Lodge, the home of Theophilus Hunter in Wake County, about four miles south of Raleigh. The news of the destruction of his powder and supplies near Concord, North Carolina, just made him even more determined to crush the Regulator movement. He had started the march of his militia troops during the last week of April 1771 from New Bern on the coast. The governor had been joined along the way by other militia, including foot troops, horsemen, artillery and rangers from the counties of Beaufort, Hanover, Craven, Onslow, Dobbs (now Lenoir), Johnston, Duplin and Wake. Most of the militia were from the eastern colonies, while the Regulators were typically from the western foothill counties. While in Wake County, the governor sent out detachments to help sheriffs collect land taxes and other fees owed the colonial government and its officers. Tryon wanted to show settlers in the area the military strength of his militia. He marched the troops to the Eno River in Orange County, a few miles from Hillsborough, and camped there on May 9. Tryon was joined by Edmund Fanning, the most hated sheriff in the province, and a detachment of the militia from Orange County. Governor Tryon had made Fanning a colonel in the militia. When the governor reached Orange County, his forces totaled 1,452 men, of whom 1,068 were from the eastern counties. At the same time, Regulators began to gather near Greensboro until they reached 2,000 strong. Tryon ordered General Hugh Waddell to march with his militia forces, which consisted of about 300 men from Bladen and Cumberland Counties, from

Salisbury to near Greensboro in Orange County, now Guilford County, and join up with the governor's troops. General Waddell originally was meant to bring the ammunition wagon train with him but was unable to do so because it had been blown up by the Mecklenburg Black Boys.

After General Waddell crossed the Yadkin River on his way toward Greensboro, he camped about two miles past the river on Potts' Creek on the evening of May 9. His troops were surrounded by Regulators, many of whom were from Mecklenburg County and had been members of Reverend Alexander Craighead's congregations. Among the officers for the Regulators was Captain Benjamin Merrill, who lived at the Jersey Settlement near Salisbury and commanded a company of more than three hundred men. A bronze plaque dedicated to Captain Benjamin Merrill is on a stone marker in downtown Lexington, North Carolina, with the words: "Sacrificed his life for the cause of the Regulators. Was executed by officials of the Crown, June 19, 1771. Home was 8 miles south." The Regulators demanded that General Waddell retreat back over the Yadkin River and threatened his troops if he should try to advance. The general found that many of his men were not willing to fight the Regulators and others actually supported the Regulators' cause. One of his captains reported that he had reviewed the strength of the Regulators and found that the foot troops were a quarter mile long and seven to eight men deep. He also reported that the horsemen were about 120 yards long and twelve to fourteen deep. The decision was made by a council of the generals' officers to retreat across the Yadkin. The general had their decision written down, and it read as follows:

> *General Waddell's Camp*
> *Potts' Creek, 10th May, 1771*
>
> *By a Council of Officers of the Western Detachment*
> *Considering the great superiority of the insurgents in number, and the resolution of a great part of their own men not to fight, it was resolved that they should retreat across the Yadkin.*

The decision was signed by ten of General Waddell's officers. After Waddell's troops retreated across the river, the Regulators pursued them back to Salisbury. Many of Waddell's men deserted along the way, and his forces were greatly reduced by the time they reached Salisbury. At that time, the general sent a messenger to Governor Tryon to warn him of their retreat.

Benjamin Merrill plaque. *Photo by author.*

Governor Tryon was already aware of the Regulators gathered near Salisbury and of another Regulator force, which had come together on the Alamance Creek about six miles south of present-day Burlington, now in Alamance and Guilford Counties. Many of the Regulators were likely from Mecklenburg County and former parishioners of Reverend Craighead, but since Regulators typically kept their identities secret, it is difficult to ascertain their names. It is certain that Robert Caruthers, Benjamin Cochran, Robert Davis and William White, son of James White, were among the Regulators. All four men were Mecklenburg Black Boys and parishioners of the Rocky River church of Reverend Craighead. Tryon decided to break camp near Hillsborough and march toward Alamance Creek. The name for the creek was derived from the old Sissipahaw Indian word *Alamons*, which meant "Noisy River."

On May 13, Governor Tryon crossed the Haw River, west of Burlington, and camped about six miles from the Regulators, who numbered about two thousand. It was reported that James Hunter, one of the leaders of the Regulators and known as the "General of the Regulators," was asked to command the men at Alamance. He refused, saying, "We are all free men and every man must command himself." On Wednesday, May 15, the Regulators sent a petition to the governor at about 6:00 p.m. that accused him of having made a preconceived judgment against their cause and was determined to destroy them. It requested that he stop his advance toward them and listen to their grievances. It asked for a response in four hours. The governor responded that he would answer by noon the next day, but he quickly decided that he would advance against the insurgents the next morning and would then present a letter to them offering his terms. If they refused, he would attack them. That evening, two of Tryon's officers, Captain Ashe and Captain John Walker, were captured outside the governor's camp by the Regulators, tied to trees, badly whipped and kept as prisoners. Many of the men on each side stayed up all night to guard against a surprise attack. Soon after 7:00 a.m. on May 16, Governor Tryon began to march his troops to the west within a few miles of the

Left: Alexander Martin. *Painting by unknown artist, circa 1793. Courtesy of the North Carolina Museum of History.*

Right: James Hunter monument. *Photo by author.*

Regulators' position. Three small brass cannons were fired, which was a signal for the troops to move into battle lines to make sure they were ready in case of an attack. After that proved successful, the men again formed a column and continued to march. At that time, Reverend David Caldwell, the son-in-law of Reverend Alexander Craighead and pastor of a Presbyterian church at nearby Alamance, along with Alexander Martin, who later became governor of North Carolina after the American Revolution, Robert Thompson and Robert Matter, called on Governor Tryon while he rode with his troops. They had also visited Tryon the day before, attempting to persuade the governor not to attack the Regulators and asking him to negotiate with the Regulators about their grievances. Reverend Caldwell had done so at the urging of his parishioners. He was able to get Tryon to promise not to attack until he had tried to negotiate—a promise the governor had no intention of keeping. The governor kept Robert Thompson and Robert Matter as prisoners and allowed Reverend Caldwell and Alexander Martin to leave. When the militia was within a half mile of the Regulators' line, a cannon was shot twice, and the militia again formed battle lines. Tryon then sent his aide-de-camp, Philmore Hawkins, and Colonel Edmund Fanning to the Regulators' position. The two men went to about four paces behind the Regulators' lines, and Colonel Fanning read the governor's letter to the surrounding men. The letter read as follows:

> *Alamance Camp, Thursday, May 16th, 1771.*
>
> *To Those Who Style Themselves "Regulators":*
>
> *In reply to your petition of yesterday, I am to acquaint you that I have been attentive to the interests of your County and to every individual residing therein. I lament the fatal necessity to which you have now reduced me by withdrawing yourselves from the mercy of the crown and from the laws of your country. To require you who are now assembled as Regulators, to quietly lay down your arms, to surrender up your leaders, to the laws of your country and rest on the leniency of the Government. By accepting these terms within one hour from the delivery of this dispatch, you will prevent an effusion of blood, as you are at this time in a state of REBELLION against your King, your country, and your laws.*
>
> [Signed]
> *William Tryon*

Whenever Fanning read the governor's letter, he was greeted with loud clamors and raucous cries. It was obvious the Regulators weren't going to obey Tryon's demands. The militia kept moving forward slowly until the two sides could see each other. Some of the Regulators moved out front of their lines and shouted at and taunted the governor's men, and then they quickly moved back into their lines. Fanning and Malcolm reported back to the governor that "the Rebels…[had] rejected the terms offer'd with distain… [saying] they wanted no time to consider of them and with rebellious clamor [*sic*] called out for battle." It is assumed that most of the Regulators didn't really believe that there would actually be a battle. Many had no weapons, and all had little ammunition. They believed that their superior numbers would make Tryon back down and negotiate with them about their grievances. Both sides advanced to within three hundred yards of each other. Reverend David Caldwell was riding up and down the Regulators' line, urging them to go home without fighting. He was finally persuaded to leave because the fighting was likely to begin soon. He actually barely escaped the battle. Officers of Tryon went to the Regulators' position in an attempt to negotiate an exchange of prisoners. They were willing to turn over seven prisoners they held, including Robert Thompson, for Captain Ashe and Captain Walker. Messengers were sent back and forth, but about 11:15 a.m., Governor Tryon began to believe that the Regulators were stalling, and he sent a second letter at noon to the Regulators by his aide-de-camp, Malcolm. The letter read:

> *Gentlemen and Regulators:*
> *Those of you who are not too far committed should desist and quietly return to your homes, those of you who have laid yourselves liable should submit without resistance. I and others promise to obtain for you the best possible terms. The Governor will grant you nothing. You are unprepared for war! You have no cannon! You have no military training! You have no commanding officers to lead you in battle. You have no ammunition. You will be defeated!*

The Regulators were still trying to get the militia to turn over the seven prisoners Tryon had promised to exchange for the two they had captured the day before. Tryon was in agreement, but after a half hour, when he didn't see the captured officers, Tryon marched his men within thirty yards of the Regulators. The Regulators began to wave their hats and dared the militia to fire on them. Tryon sent another message "cautioning the Rebels to take care of themselves, as he should immediately give the signal for action!" The Regulators' reply was: "Fire and be damned."

After the Regulators' taunts of Tryon's army, Robert Thompson attempted to escape by riding toward the Regulators' position. Governor Tryon pulled out his pistol and shot him dead in plain view of many of the Regulators. Tryon then sent out a white flag of truce, but the Regulators, having seen the shooting of Thompson, fired on the flag. The lines came closer and closer until they almost met. The governor gave an order to the cannoneers to fire an attack signal, but they hesitated for a time. The governor gave the order again with more force. The five cannons were finally fired. The militia didn't start firing its rifles immediately, so Tryon yelled, "Fire!" and the men still hesitated. The Regulators dared them to fire. "Fire!" yelled the governor again, "Fire! On them or on me!" The militia began firing by platoons. The Regulators returned fire in a haphazard manner from behind trees and rocks. Some brave young Regulators rushed forward and snatched one of the militia's cannons but, not knowing how to operate it, quickly abandoned the cannon and dropped back behind their lines. The Regulators were very disorganized, with no officers, no discipline and many without weapons and little ammunition. They fired as individuals against a cohesive force. But they refused to run until they had expended all the ammunition they did have. The firings of the Regulators began to slow down as they ran out of ammunition; the militia began to advance into the trees, and the Regulators began to flee. The Battle of Alamance lasted two hours, and by 2:30 p.m., almost all the Regulators had fled. The militiamen captured about fifteen prisoners, and once they were behind the Regulators' lines, they found seventy saddlebags with ammunition and supplies. Nine Regulators and twenty-seven militiamen had been killed. More than one hundred Regulators were wounded, but most escaped, and sixty-one militiamen were wounded. Captain Benjamin Merrill and his men had been only a day's march away from Alamance and heard the cannons firing but weren't able to get there in time. He deeply regretted not being able to participate. Many Regulator sympathizers believed that he and his three hundred men could have made a big difference to the Regulators. He could have acted as their commanding officer and coordinated their efforts.

The Battle of Alamance took place almost four years before the well-known Battles of Lexington and Concord, and the North Carolina battle deserves to be considered the first battle of the Revolutionary War. It was fought for different reasons than the battles in Massachusetts on April 19, 1775, but both were acts of rebellion against British authority. The militiamen in Lexington and Concord had learned that the British intended to capture and destroy military supplies stored at Concord. The intent of the militiamen was to protect their property. They were not making an announcement of independence from England. That wouldn't be done until over a year later. It was simply an act of rebellion against British authority. The same was true in North Carolina. The North Carolina governor and his council were appointed by officials of the king of England and as such were representatives of the Crown, as were the local county officials who collected taxes for the colony. In rebelling against the corrupt tax system of North Carolina, the Regulators were rebelling against the British Crown just as much as the Patriots in Massachusetts were rebelling against the British Crown. As Governor Tryon stated in his letter, which was read to the Regulators by Colonel Fanning just before the Battle of Alamance, "You are at this time in a state of rebellion against your King." The Battles of Lexington and Concord are historically considered to be the first battles of the Revolutionary War because they were the "first open armed conflicts between the Kingdom of Great Britain and its colonies in British North America." The Battle of Alamance was obviously an "open armed conflict," and although the Massachusetts battles were against British army regulars, the militiamen gathered by the royal governor were definitely representing the British Crown. As the royal governor himself wrote, the Regulators were considered to be "in a state of rebellion against your King." In one way, the Regulators at Alamance were more rebellious than the Patriots at Lexington and Concord because the Regulators were rebelling against the corrupt British tax collection process that supported the royal governor and the British system of governance in their colony. The Massachusetts Patriots were merely trying to protect their military supplies from the British. The Regulators were the aggressors, while the men at Lexington and Concord were defenders. The number of combatants in each of the conflicts was large, but the Regulators actually had more casualties than the Massachusetts Patriots—109 killed and wounded as opposed to 88 killed or wounded. Both conflicts were fought before the colonies declared a national declaration of independence. President William McKinley believed the Battle of Alamance was the first battle of the Revolutionary War. In a speech in 1893, when he was governor of Ohio, he was speaking of the Alamance conflict and stated, "They were the first to proclaim for freedom in these United States; even before Lexington the Scotch-Irish blood had been shed for American freedom." The Battle of Alamance deserves to be thought of as the first battle of the Revolutionary War.

Above: Battle of Alamance monument. *Photo by author.*

Right: Detail on Battle of Alamance monument, a tribute to the first battle of the Revolution. *Photo by author.*

Following the Battle of Alamance, the wounded Regulators and the wounded militiamen were placed in wagons and taken back to Tryon's camp near Burlington. The unwounded prisoners were marched in chains. At the camp, Tryon's surgeon treated all the wounded, including the Regulators. Under the Johnston Riot Act passed in January 1771, all the Regulators were considered rebels who could immediately be put to death. The militiamen were urging that this be done because twenty-seven of their friends and fellow soldiers had been killed by the Regulators and many more wounded. After the funerals of the dead militiamen on Friday evening, May 17, the prisoner James Few, a slow-witted young carpenter who lived near Hillsborough, was hanged without a trial. James Few had joined the Regulators because he had been affected by the illegal taxes and fees extracted from him by Sheriff Fanning and by a dishonor done to his intended bride by Fanning. When he became a Regulator, he declared that he had been "sent by heaven to release the world of oppression, and to begin in Carolina." Governor Tryon not only had Few hanged but also later destroyed provisions made for Few's parents. Governor Tryon announced on the same day, May 17, that he would be making proclamations of pardon to all Regulators with a number of exceptions if they would swear loyalty to the government. The official proclamations were made over the next month with the June 9, 1771 proclamation as follows:

> *A Proclamation. Whereas Herman Husband, James Hunter, Rednap Howell and William Butler are Outlawed and liable to be shot by any Person whatsoever, I do therefore, that they be punished for the Traterous* [sic] *and Rebellious Crimes they have committed, issue this my Proclamation hereby offering a Reward of One Hundred Pounds and one thousand acres of Land to any Person or Persons who will take Dead or Alive and bring into mine or General Waddell's Camp either and each of the above named outlaws. Given under my Hand and the great Seal of the said Province at Bathabara this ninth day of June in the year of our Lord 1771.*
>
> [signed]
> *Wm. Tryon*
> *By His excellency's command Js. Edwards, P. Sec.*

The proclamation of June 11, 1771, was as follows:

> *A Proclamation. Whereas I am informed that many Persons who have been concerned in the late Rebellion are desirous of submitting themselves to*

> *Government, I do therefore give Notice that every Person who will come in either to mine or General Waddell's Camp, lay down their Arms, take the Oath of Allegiance and promise to pay all Taxes that are now due or may hereafter become due by them respectively and submit to the Laws of this Country shall have His Majesty's most Gracious and Free Pardon for all the Treasons, Insurrections and Rebellions done or committed on or before the Sixteenth of May last. Provided they make their submission aforesaid on or before the Tenth of July next; the following Persons are however excepted for the Benefit of this Proclamation Viz, all the Outlaws, the Prisoners, all those concerned in blowing up General Waddell Ammunition in Mecklenburg County...Given under my Hand and the Great Seal of the Province, this eleventh day of June A. Dom. 1771.*
>
> [signed]
> *Wm. Tryon*
> *God save the King*

With this proclamation, Tryon excepted the Mecklenburg Black Boys from the pardon. Following the governor's announcement of May 17 concerning the forthcoming proclamations of pardon, some detachments of the militia searched the countryside for the next few days looking for Regulator leaders. Some of the leaders, such as Herman Husband, Rednap Howell, James Hunter and William Butler, had fled the colony. Also on May 17, the Regulator prisoner Captain Messer was sentenced to be hanged the next day. When she heard her husband was a prisoner and had been condemned to die, Captain Messer's wife came to the camp with her ten-year-old son to plead with Governor Tryon for her husband's life. Tryon wasn't moved even when she wept uncontrollably, lying on the ground with her son weeping by her side. Then the boy stepped up to the governor and said, "Sir, hang me and let my father live!" The governor asked, "Who told you to say that!?" "Nobody!" said the boy. Then the governor questioned, "And why do you ask that?" The lad answered, "Because if you hang my father, my mother will die and the children will perish." "Well! Your father shall not be hung today," the governor replied. Colonel Edmund Fanning suggested that Captain Messer be given his freedom if he could bring back Herman Husband, while Messer's wife and son were kept as hostages. Captain Messer searched for Herman Husband for the next few days and actually found him in Virginia but couldn't bring him back. When Messer returned to the camp without Husband, he was put in chains and made a prisoner again.

On May 19, a Sunday, the Regulators attacked a sentry post of the militia before daybreak, wounding one sentry and taking another prisoner. On May 21, Tryon's army marched to the farm of James Hunter, one of the Regulator leaders, near present-day Liberty, now in Guilford County, and burned down his house and outbuildings. In the evening of the same day, they marched to the plantation of Herman Husband near Sandy Creek in present-day Siler City, now in Chatham County. The governor took ownership of the plantation, but Herman Husband could not be found. General Waddell left his militia at the Yadkin River and joined Tryon at Sandy Creek on May 31. Colonel Fanning and his detachment captured Captain Benjamin Merrill and brought him to the Sandy Creek camp on June 1, and Merrill was put into chains along with the other prisoners. Governor Tryon then marched his troops westward up to the Yadkin River, making a great display of the prisoners to the inhabitants along the route, announcing the pardon for the rebels and demanding that they all take an oath of allegiance. The governor camped at Captain Merrill's plantation near Salisbury and was joined there by Waddell's militia, which had marched north from south of the Yadkin River. All of Tryon's horsemen had pastured their horses on the plantation and allowed them to roam freely but with bells around their necks so they could be easily found. About midnight on June 1, a number of militiamen raided some beehives on the plantation near where the horses were located. One of the hives got knocked over, and the angry bees attacked the horses. The frightened horses broke through a fence and ran through the camp, making loud distress noises with their bells clanging. The sleeping militiamen were startled awake, grabbed their rifles and prepared themselves for what they thought was a surprise Regulator attack. The journal writer for Tryon wrote of the incident, "This consternation…cast more horror on the waking imagination than anything else that happened during the whole service!" While encamped at Merrill's plantation, the governor sent General Waddell with a company of twenty-five horsemen, one piece of artillery and a corps of militia to the counties in the south and west to make the announcement of pardons and request oaths of allegiance.

Tryon then headed back east, parading the chained prisoners through the villages near the route and made all the inhabitants he encountered give an oath of allegiance. He administered the oath of allegiance to over six thousand settlers on the march back to Hillsborough. He also made anyone he suspected of being a Regulator provide provisions for his troops, and he took supplies from houses that he found unoccupied. Tryon also arrested a man named Johnson who had previously insulted the sister of the

James Hunter marker. *Photo by author.*

governor's wife, a woman called Lady Wake, after whom Wake County had been named. The governor had Johnson given 250 lashes on his back and released. As he headed back east, Tryon enjoyed burning houses, destroying crops and holding court-martials for civil crimes. On June 14, the army arrived in Hillsborough on the date a special court had been ordered by the governor to try the fourteen prisoners traveling with his army under the provisions of the Johnston Riot Act.

The court was conducted by Chief Justice Martin Howard and Associate Justices Maurice Moore, who was the father of future U.S. Supreme Court justice Alfred Moore, and Richard Henderson. A jury tried the Regulators on charges of high treason. Reverend David Caldwell traveled forty-six miles by horseback from Alamance to testify to the character of the men he knew, who included Robert Matter and Robert Thompson, and to comfort them with his counsel and prayers. Twelve of the men were found guilty and stood in front of Judge Howard to hear their fates. Howard read the following sentence for high treason against the Crown:

> *I must now close my afflicting duty, by pronouncing upon you the awful Sentence of the Law; which is that you...be carried to the place from whence you came, that you be drawn from thence to the Place of Execution, where you are to be hanged by the Neck; that you be cut down while yet alive, that your Bowels be taken out and burnt before your Face, that your Head be cut off, your Body divided into Four Quarters, and this to be at his Majesty's Disposal; and the Lord have Mercy on your Soul.*

The men wouldn't actually have their bowels cut out while still alive, their heads cut off or their bodies quartered. That part of the sentence hadn't been executed in England for centuries, but they would be hanged. Governor Tryon then pardoned six of the twelve men found guilty, hoping that he would be perceived as being benevolent by the western settlers. The six pardoned men were Forest Mercer, James Stewart, Herman Cox, James Emerson, William Brown and James Copeland. But the governor became very upset that the remaining six weren't executed right away, and he sent his aide-de-camp to the judges to threaten them.

They weren't hanged until five days later, on June 19, just outside the town of Hillsborough, a short distance from the Eno River. Governor Tryon had made a parade out of the affair, marching many in his army around the men to be hanged with his horsemen on the outside to keep the crowd away. Those hanged were Captain Benjamin Merrill, Captain Messer, Robert Matter, James Pugh and two other Regulators whose names are not known. Robert Matter had escaped being hanged a month and a day from the date he was originally scheduled to die by the actions of his son, but now his time had run out. Robert Matter had never joined the Regulators but had accompanied Reverend David Caldwell, Alexander Martin and Robert Thompson to Governor Tryon's camp at Alamance to persuade the governor to negotiate with the Regulators. Matter had been recognized by Tryon as someone who had offended the governor sometime in the past with a letter that was entrusted to Matter's care and because of that had kept him as a prisoner. James Pugh, a brother-in-law of Herman Husband, had killed fifteen of the artillery men with his rifle during the Battle of Alamance but had waited too long to make his escape and had been captured. When he was placed under the gallows, standing on top of a barrel, he asked Tryon for a half hour to speak, which the governor granted. He said he was justified in what he had done, he was ready to meet God and told the crowd that "His blood would be as good seed sown on good ground which would produce an hundredfold." He declared that the Regulators had taken no man's life before the battle and had wanted nothing other than the correcting of their grievances. He then spoke against the corruption of public officers, particularly that of Sheriff Fanning. At which point, Fanning signaled to one of his men to tip over the barrel Pugh was standing on. Pugh was the first to be hanged and never got to finish his allotted time to speak. A plaque depicting James Pugh about to be hanged and the words he spoke is on the James Hunter monument at the Battle of Alamance site. Captain Benjamin Merrill was permitted to speak and declared:

James Pugh plaque. *Photo by author.*

> *I received by the grace of God, a change fifteen years ago; but have, since that time, been a backslider; yet Providence, which is my chief security, has been pleased to give me comfort, under these evils, in my last hour; and altho' the halter is now round my neck, believe me, I would not change stations with any man on the ground. All you, who think you stand, take heed lest ye fall. I would be glad to say a few words more to you before I die. In a few moments, I shall leave widow and ten children; I entreat that no reflection may be cast upon them on my account; and if possible, shall deem it as a bounty, should you, gentlemen petition the Governor and Council, that some part of my estate may be spared for the widow and fatherless; it will be an act of charity, for I have forfeited the whole, by the laws of God and man.*

As he was about to be hanged, Captain Merrill began to devoutly sing a psalm, and one of Tryon's militiamen remarked that if all men went to the gallows as Merrill had, "hanging would be an honorable death." Then the remaining four condemned men were hanged. Behind the parking lot of the Orange County Board of Education building in Hillsboro is a four- by

Plaque commemorating the Regulators hanged. *Photo by author.*

eight-foot iron fence marking the place where the Regulators were hanged. Within the fence is a bronze plaque on a stone marker with the words: "On this spot were hanged by order of a Tory court—June 19, 1771—Merrill, Messer, Matter, Pugh and two other Regulators."

Judge Maurice Moore was disgusted by Governor's Tryon's parade approach to the hangings and wrote to him shortly afterward, signing the name "Atticus." The letter included this reprimand: "The Governor's minute and personal attention to these particulars left a ridiculous idea of his character behind him, bearing a strong resemblance to that of the undertaker at a funeral. These brave men whose only sin was having warred against corruption and oppression, deserved a different fate; but Tryon was not like Fingal, who never injured the brave, though his arm was strong."

Fingal, the strong king of Morven in an ancient epic poem, could have easily killed the fallen Orla, whose shield Fingal had broken in two, but because of Orla's bravery, he didn't slay him. Soon after the hangings, Governor Tryon left for New Bern because he had been notified by the king's officials that he'd been appointed governor of New York. He left North Carolina for New York on June 30, 1771.

The actions of Reverend Craighead's parishioners in the War of Sugar Creek and the blowing up of the British ammunition wagon train near Concord by the Mecklenburg Black Boys emboldened the Regulators to believe they could stand up against the British authorities in North Carolina and led to the Battle of Alamance. Reverend Alexander Craighead deserves to be remembered as America's earliest revolutionary.

Chapter 7

THE MECKLENBURG DECLARATION OF INDEPENDENCE AND RESOLVES

Governor William Tryon's defeat of the Regulators at the Battle of Alamance and the hangings of six Regulators in Hillsborough had effectively put a stop to Regulator uprisings. There were still grievances among settlers about corruption in the collection of land taxes and other fees, but demonstrations against colonial authorities had almost ceased because of fears of reprisals. The assembly had provided relief regarding the Marriage Act by allowing Presbyterian ministers and other denominations besides Anglican ministers to perform marriages, but the Scotch-Irish Presbyterians still had to pay taxes to support the Anglican churches under the Vestry Act. Another grievance for the Mecklenburg inhabitants was the rescinding of an act agreed to by the North Carolina Assembly in December 1770. Meeting in New Bern, the assembly passed an act "for founding, establishing, and endowing of Queens College in the town of Charlotte," but King George III and his council reversed the decision a few months later. The council believed that, because Queens College essentially was a Presbyterian school, it would encourage dissenters from the Church of England and give more reasons for rebellion against the royalist government. It was true that many trustees of the college were Presbyterians, including Abraham Alexander, an elder at the Sugaw Creek church, and Hezekiah Alexander and John McKnitt Alexander, both elders at the Hopewell church. Dr. Ephraim Brevard, an elder at the Hopewell church, was a professor of science and medicine. They were all former parishioners of Reverend Alexander Craighead, a known great dissenter among dissenters. The assembly passed the act a second time in 1771, but again it was repealed by royal proclamation, this time announced by the new governor of North Carolina, Josiah Martin. When Tryon left to become governor of New York in June 1771, Martin had been appointed by the king's officials to take his place. Even without a charter, Queens College continued to thrive, though the lack of a charter made it more difficult to secure operational funds. The school, which had about eighty students, soon became a center for debates about freedom and independence from England.

Governor Josiah Martin of North Carolina. *Courtesy of the State Archives of North Carolina.*

The inhabitants of Mecklenburg had hoped that Governor Martin would prove to be an improvement over Governor Tryon, but in many ways, Martin was found to be even more arrogant and intolerant than his predecessor. Governor Martin closed the land office on June 28, 1773, by order of the king's council, and rumors started in the province that it was the intention of the Crown to get the British Parliament to vacate all American land titles by voiding former patents, causing the titles to revert back to the Crown. The Court of Claims continued to remain open until February 1775, and patents based on old entries, warrants and surveys were issued, while all applications for new entries and warrants were denied. This caused even more anxiety among the province's inhabitants about the Crown and the royal government. Governor Martin began to meet strong resistance from the North Carolina Assembly, especially the Whigs in the legislature, concerning how the colony should be administered, and he began to secretly organize the Loyalist elements in the province.

The governor tried to prevent the formation of the Provincial Congress in North Carolina, an illegal assembly, independent of the British colonial government, but he was unable to stop its meetings. North Carolina was the first colony to have a Provincial Congress meet in defiance of British orders, and it held its initial meeting on August 25–27, 1774, at the Tryon Palace in New Bern. Its moderator was John Harvey, who was also the Speaker of the House of Commons of the North Carolina Assembly, and it had seventy-one delegates from thirty of the thirty-six counties, most of whom were also assemblymen. The Provincial Congress approved the calling of the first Continental Congress, which met in Philadelphia from September 5 to October 26, 1774, and had fifty-six delegates from twelve of the thirteen colonies. The Provincial Congress elected Richard Caswell, Joseph Hewes and William Hooper as North Carolina's delegates to the national Congress.

In 1775, came the shocking news that on February 9, both houses of the British Parliament, in a joint address to King George III, had declared the colonies to be in a state of rebellion and approved all necessary means, including force, to compel the colonists to obey the laws of the British government.

Governor Martin called a meeting of the North Carolina Assembly to begin on April 3, 1775, and the Provincial Congress decided to meet at the same time and place with almost the same membership. The governor made a speech to the assembly, denouncing its actions, and laid out his position in strong terms, and the assembly responded to him with equally strong language. The governor dissolved the assembly on April 8, and he never called it again. On April 24, 1775, while Governor Martin was in session with members of his council, a group of Whigs attacked his house and took away six guns he had stored there. The next day, he sent his family to New York and took refuge at Fort Johnston on the Cape Fear River.

On August 23, 1775, after news of the Battle of Bunker Hill in Boston, King George III issued a proclamation of rebellion officially titled "A Proclamation for Suppressing Rebellion and Sedition" that declared elements of the American colonies in a state of "open and avowed rebellion" and ordered officials of the British Empire "to use their utmost endeavors to withstand and suppress such rebellion."

For years, the leading men of Mecklenburg County had met at the cotton plantation of John McKnitt Alexander, called Alexandriana, in present-day Huntersville to discuss the events of the day and politics. Reverend Alexander Craighead had been a frequent guest at these meetings, and he used the meetings as opportunities to once again advocate independence from England and resistance to colonial authorities. The gathering also included Dr. Ephraim Brevard; Hezekiah Alexander; Waightstill Avery, a boarder at Hezekiah Alexander's house; and Abraham Alexander. In the years since Reverend Craighead's death, the meetings included Reverend Hezekiah James Balch, the new pastor at the Rocky River and Poplar Tent churches. They met at a spring on the plantation and sat on logs. The host typically served potent drinks, such as corn liquor and apple brandy, which he had distilled on his property. In 1775, a lot of discussions centered on the oppressions of the North Carolina inhabitants by the Crown and events that had occurred in other colonies, such as the Boston Massacre and Boston Tea Party and, most recently, the closing of the Boston Port by the British Parliament on March 30, 1774. Reports were coming from the North that Boston was short of food because of the British occupation, and the men were discussing sending one hundred beef cattle to Boston for relief. It was decided at one of the meetings to ask Colonel Thomas Polk, who had been appointed by the North Carolina Assembly to lead the Mecklenburg Militia, along with Adam Alexander as lieutenant colonel, to oversee the selection of two delegates from each of the Mecklenburg Militia companies for a county convention. After the delegates were selected by each of the companies, it was agreed that the convention would start in the evening of May 19, 1775, at the log county courthouse.

There was great excitement on the day of Mecklenburg's first convention, which evolved into a frenzied passion when an express rider brought news of the Battles of Lexington and Concord that had occurred exactly one month earlier, on April 19. The convention elected Abraham Alexander as chairman and John McKnitt Alexander as clerk and keeper of the convention's minutes. Both men were elders in Reverend Craighead's former churches. A resolutions committee was appointed, made up of Dr. Ephraim Brevard, an elder in Reverend Craighead's former Hopewell church; Reverend Hezekiah James Balch; and William Kennon, a lawyer from Salisbury, forty miles to the north of Charlotte. The committee was to write any resolutions

Signers plaque at Alexandriana, the birthplace of the Mecklenburg Declaration of Independence. *Photo by author.*

News of the Battles of Lexington and Concord. *Illustration in* The Revolution in North Carolina, *1916, by Archibald Henderson.*

that the convention might approve. The bloodshed at Lexington and Concord caused delegates to shout out, "Let us be independent! Let us declare our independence, and defend it with our lives and fortunes!" The delegates expressed their conviction that the actions of Parliament, in stating that the colonies were in a state of rebellion, meant that the colonies were out of the protection of the British Crown and that they should declare themselves out of the king's control. Dr. Ephraim Brevard had drawn up some resolutions before the convention and had read them to his friends at a political meeting at Queens College. He read them again to the delegates of the convention, first stating that he was committed to having the other two men on the resolutions committee make revisions to them. The resolutions included language about independence from England, and one delegate addressed Chairman Abraham Alexander, stating, "If you resolve on Independence, how shall we all be absolved from the obligations of the oath we took to be true to King George the Third, about four years ago, after the Regulation battle, when we were sworn, whole militia companies together? I should be glad to know how gentlemen can clear their consciences after taking that oath?"

The delegate was speaking of the Battle of Alamance and the bloodshed caused by Governor Tryon on May 16, 1771, and the oath of allegiance forced on the people by the governor to save their lives and property. The question created a lot of confusion, and so many people tried to speak that the chairman had trouble keeping order. It seemed that unless the question was answered satisfactorily, there wouldn't be a vote for independence. One of the delegates stated that "allegiance and protection were reciprocal; when protection was withdrawn, allegiance ceased; that the oath was binding only while the King protected us in our rights and liberties as they existed at the time taken." Some responded to this idea as being "Nonsense!" Another delegate seemed to persuade the assembly with an analogy when he pointed to a green tree next to the courthouse and declared, "If I am sworn to do a thing as long as the leaves continue on that tree, I am bound by that oath as long as the leaves continue. But when the leaves fall, I am released from that obligation." Another delegate stated that an oath made under the threat of death should not be considered binding. The convention seemed to have decided that when protection

Rough notes of John McKnitt Alexander. *Courtesy of the Southern Historical Collection, Wilson Library, University of North Carolina.*

ceased, allegiance also ceased and the delegates enacted an outline of a declaration, which the resolutions committee was to write. About 2:00 a.m., the convention adjoined until the next day.

The convention reconvened at noon on May 20, 1775, with a multitude of people assembled on the outside of the courthouse, including wives and mothers, awaiting the final outcome with great anticipation. The resolutions that had been revised by the full resolutions committee of Dr. Brevard, Reverend Balch and William Kennon were read to the convention by Dr. Brevard. It included a declaration of independence from Great Britain. The chairman, John McKnitt Alexander, asked the delegates, "Are you all agreed?" The answer was a unanimous "aye." The convention then agreed that the Mecklenburg Declaration of Independence should be read to the multitude of people waiting outside the courthouse by Colonel Thomas Polk. When Colonel Polk read the declaration, it was received with great excitement and approval by the people outside the courthouse, who whooped and hollered and threw their hats into the air. The Mecklenburg Declaration of Independence was not seen again until it appeared forty-four years later in an article in the *Raleigh Register* on April 30, 1819. It is likely that the language used in the declaration became embellished over that period of time and that the rough notes of the declaration kept by John McKnitt Alexander are closer to the essential meaning of the original document. His rough notes were as follows:

> *1st. We (the County) by a solemn and awfull* [sic] *vote, Dissolved (abjured) our allegiance to King George and the British Nation.*
>
> *2d. Declared ourselves a free & independent people, having a right and capable to govern ourselves (as part of North Carolina).*
>
> *3d. In order to have laws as a rule of life for our future Government we formed a Code of laws; by adopting our former wholesome laws.*
>
> *4th. And as there was then no officers Civil or Military in our County we decreed that every Militia officer in said County should hold and occupy his former commission and grade. And that every member present of this Committee shall henceforth* [act] *as a Justice of the peace, in the character of a Committee man* [to] *hear and determine all controversies agreeable to said laws* [margin torn] *peace, union & harmony in said County—and to use every* [margin torn] *spread the Electrical fire of freedom among ourselves &* [margin torn, words missing].
>
> *5th. etc., etc. Many other laws and ordinances were then ma*[de].

The language of the declaration read to the convention and to the public outside the courthouse would have been more elegant, but Alexander's rough notes provide the best source about the content of the declaration. Because the declaration was not published until 1819 and due to the confusion over its exact wording, its authenticity became very controversial and remains so even today.

There were twenty-seven signers of the Mecklenburg Declaration of Independence. Of that total, nineteen were known to be members of the seven Presbyterian churches where Reverend Alexander Craighead was the pastor, and one attended a gathering of Presbyterians at Clear Creek to which Reverend Craighead was a missionary minister. That gathering became the Philadelphia Presbyterian Church in 1770. Of those twenty men, eleven were elders of Reverend Craighead's churches. Of the remaining seven signers, Thomas Polk was married to the former Susannah Spratt, who, along with the entire Spratt family, was a member of the Steele Creek church, and Thomas Polk's daughter Margaret married Dr. Ephraim Brevard, who was an elder of the Hopewell church. Thomas Polk was obviously very aware of Reverend Craighead's preaching about independence from Great Britain and resistance to colonial authorities. It was reported that Charles Alexander was an unbeliever in the Christian religion, but he was the brother of Adam Alexander, an elder at the Rocky River church. Charles would also have been well aware of Reverend Craighead's preaching on independence. Ezra Alexander might have attended one of Reverend Craighead's churches since his son Augustus Alexander later became a member of the Sharon Presbyterian Church in Charlotte, which was organized in 1830. Reverend Hezekiah James Balch had followed Reverend Craighead as minister of the Rocky River and Polar Tent churches and obviously knew of his preachings. Waightstill Avery lived with Hezekiah Alexander, who was an

Mecklenburg Declaration monument. *Photo by author.*

elder of the Hopewell church. Avery could well have attended the Hopewell church, and it is certain that Avery attended the meetings at John McKnitt Alexander's plantation, at which Reverend Craighead often spoke of independence from Great Britain. William Kennon was an Anglican lawyer from Salisbury, forty miles to the north. The other signer not known to have attended one of Reverend Craighead's churches, William Graham, was an Irishman. The twenty Scotch-Irish Presbyterians, who were known members of Reverend Craighead's seven churches and the Presbyterian gathering at Clear Creek, are as follows, along with their church membership:

- Abraham Alexander (chairman)—elder, Sugaw Creek church
- Adam Alexander—elder, Rocky River church
- Hezekiah Alexander—elder, Hopewell church
- John McKnitt Alexander (secretary)—elder, Hopewell church
- Richard Barry—elder, Hopewell church
- Ephraim Brevard—elder, Hopewell church
- John Davidson—Hopewell church
- Henry Downs—Providence church
- John Flenniker—Providence church
- John Foard—Rocky River church
- James Harris—Presbyterian gathering at Clear Creek (became Philadelphia Presbyterian Church in 1770)
- Robert Harris Sr.—elder, Poplar Tent church
- Robert Irwin—Steele Creek church
- Matthew McClure—elder, Hopewell church
- Neill Morrison—Providence church
- Benjamin Patton—Poplar Tent church
- John Phifer—elder, Rocky River church
- John Queary—elder, Rocky River church
- David Reese—elder, Poplar Tent church
- Zaccheus Wilson Sr.—elder, Steele Creek church

There were six signers of the declaration with the last name Alexander, all members of one of the largest clans in Mecklenburg County, and the signers were all closely related. John McKnitt and Hezekiah were brothers, sons of James. Abraham and Ezra were brothers, sons of Elias and first cousins of John McKnitt and Hezekiah. Adam and Charles were brothers, sons of William, who was another brother of Abraham and Ezra. All the Alexanders were brothers, first cousins or uncles/nephews of the other Alexanders. The

Right: Plaque commemorating Major John Davidson, a signer of the Mecklenburg Declaration of Independence. *Photo by author.*

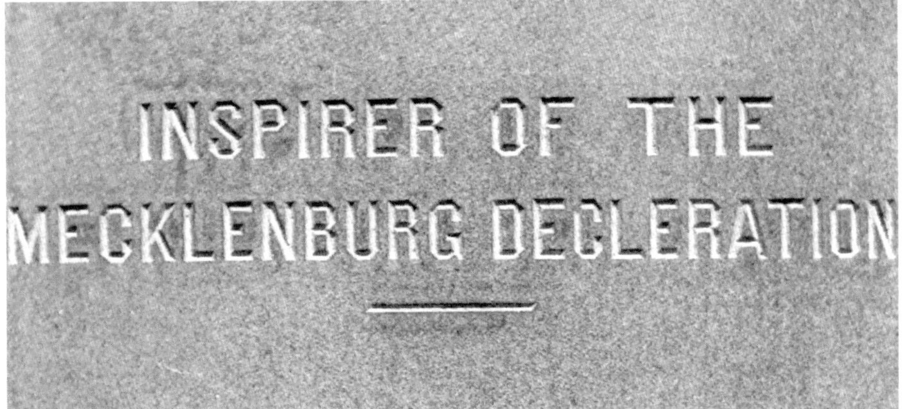

Below: Detail on monument to Reverend Craighead, inspirer of the Mecklenburg Declaration. *Photo by author.*

convention was dominated by former parishioners of Reverend Alexander Craighead, and since it was well known that he preached independence from Great Britain, he became known as "the father of the Mecklenburg Declaration of Independence" even though he wasn't alive at the time of its signing.

The rough notes of John McKnitt Alexander explain why the Mecklenburg Declaration of Independence wasn't published until 1819, over forty years after its signing. At the bottom of the first page of the notes, a paragraph states with some words torn off and the likely missing words filled in: "Allowing the 19th May to be a rash Act, [adoption of our resolutions had good] effects in binding all the middle & western [patriots together in the common cause, all] firm Whigs—not Tories but…"

The passion generated by learning of the bloodshed at Lexington and Concord had led the delegates to what was considered a rash act of declaring independence from England after only a night's reflection. It was also likely that some of the more conservative inhabitants of Mecklenburg County voiced their displeasure the next day about not being represented at the convention. There was also the natural fear that the delegates could be arrested and hanged for their rebellious actions as had been done to Regulators four years earlier. For all these reasons, it was decided not to publish the declaration, even though it had been read to the large crowd outside the courthouse.

The convention then proceeded to discuss a plan of temporary government, and an outline of the plan was agreed to by the delegates. A Committee of Safety was selected that included Abraham Alexander, Hezekiah Alexander, John McKnitt Alexander, Dr. Ephraim Brevard and Thomas Polk. One of the purposes of the committee was to put into writing the agreed upon plan in the form of resolves. Dr. Brevard was made clerk of the committee. The committee drew up the Mecklenburg Resolves over the next eleven days, and the document was agreed to by the Committee of Safety on May 31. The preamble to the Resolves makes a very strong statement that all the laws coming from the king and Parliament are annulled and vacated, and for that reason the county needed its own constitution, which was a very rebellious act in and of itself but not quite a declaration of independence. The Mecklenburg Resolves were published in the *South-Carolina Gazette* and *Country Journal* (Charles Town) on June 13,1775; the *North-Carolina Gazette* (New Bern) on June 16, 1775; and the *Cape-Fear Mercury* (Wilmington) on June 23, 1775. The document read as follows:

> *Charlotte Town, Mecklenburg County, May 31, 1775.*
>
> *This day the Committee of this County met, and passed the following RESOLVES:*
>
> *WHEREAS by an address presented to his Majesty by both Houses of Parliament in February last, the American Colonies are declared to be in a state of actual Rebellion, we conceive that all Laws and Commissions confirmed by, or derived from the Authority of the King or Parliament, are annulled and vacated, and the former civil Constitution of these Colonies for the present wholly suspended. To provide in some Degree for the*

Convention committee heads plaque. *Photo by author.*

Exigencies of the County in the present alarming Period, we deem it proper and necessary to pass resolves, viz.

1. That all Commissions, civil and military, heretofore granted by the Crown, to be exercised in these Colonies are null and void, and the Constitution of each particular Colony wholly suspended.

2. That the Provincial Congress of each Province, under the Direction of the Great Continental Congress, is invested with all legislative and executive Powers within their respective Provinces; and that no other Legislative or Executive does or can exist, at this Time, in any of these Colonies.

3. As all former Laws are now suspended in this Province, and the Congress have not provided others, we judge it necessary, for the better Preservation of good Order, to form certain Rules and Regulations for the internal Government of this County, until Laws shall be provided for us by the Congress.

4. That the inhabitants of this County do meet on a certain Day appointed by this Committee, and having formed themselves into nine companies, to wit, eight for the County, and one for the Town of Charlotte, do choose a Colonel, and other military Officers, who shall hold and exercise their several Powers by Virtue of this Choice, and independent of Great Britain, and former Constitution of this Province.

5. That for the better Preservation of the Peace, and Administration of Justice, each of these Companies do choose from their own Body two discreet Freeholders, who shall be empowered each by himself, and singly, to decide and determine all Matters of Controversy arising within the said Company under the sum of Twenty Shillings, and jointly and together all Controversies under the sum of Forty Shillings, yet so as their Decisions may admit of Appeals to the Convention of the Select Men of the whole County; and also, that any one of these shall have power to examine, and commit to Confinement, Persons accused of Petit Larceny.

6. That those two Select Men, thus chosen, do, jointly and together, choose from the Body of their particular Company two Persons, properly qualified to serve as Constables, who may assist them in the execution of their Office.

7–20. (Deals with complaints, matters of controversy, selection of a clerk, warrants, orders for sale, quitrents, public and county taxes, application of monies, officer commissions, damages, enemies, obedience to Resolves, regulation of jurisprudence, arms, and accoutrements.)

Eph. Brevard, Clerk of the Committee.
Signed by order of the Committee.

In early June, Captain James Jack, who was an elder in the Providence church and a former parishioner of Reverend Craighead, carried the Mecklenburg Declaration of Independence and the Mecklenburg Resolves by horseback to the North Carolina delegates at the Continental Congress in Philadelphia. The delegates were Richard Caswell, William Hooper and Joseph Hewes, and Captain Jack delivered the documents to them on or before June 23, 1775. Captain Jack had been asked by the convention to get Congress to sanction or approve the documents, but he returned with a letter from the three delegates thanking the Mecklenburg convention delegates for their "zeal, perseverance, order & forbearance," telling them that the declaration was premature. Even though the North Carolina delegates to the Continental Congress had chosen to not present the documents to the Congress, it seems likely that they would have discussed their contents with many of the other delegates. This would have emboldened those delegates who were leaning toward independence from England.

Captain James Jack statue. *Photo by author.*

When Governor Josiah Martin read the June 23 edition of the *Cape-Fear Mercury* with the Mecklenburg Resolves, he was outraged and alarmed. He was at that time a refugee from the governor's palace in New Bern and staying at Fort Johnson at the mouth of the Cape Fear River. He wrote to his superior in London, the Second Earl of Dartmouth, William Legge, the colonial secretary, on June 30, 1775, enclosed the newspaper and stated:

> *The Resolves of the Committee of Mecklenburg which your Lordship will find in the enclosed Newspaper [Cape-Fear Mercury], surpass all the horrid and treasonable publications that the inflammatory spirits of this Continent have yet produced, and your Lordship may depend its Authors and Abettors will not escape my due notice whenever my hands are sufficiently strengthened to attempt the recovery of the lost authority of Government. A copy of these Resolves I am informed were sent off by express to the Congress at Philadelphia as soon as they were passed in the Committee.*

Martin also asked in his letter to William Legge if he could raise a battalion of one thousand Highlanders and be given back his rank of lieutenant colonel. He bemoaned his present circumstances with the words: "The situation in which I find myself at present is indeed my Lord most despicable and mortifying…I daily see indignantly the Sacred Majesty of my Royal Master insulted, the Rights of the Crown defied and violated, his government set at naught and trampled upon."

Second Earl of Dartmouth, William Legge. *Painting by Pompeo Batoni, 1752–1756, Hood Museum of Art, Dartmouth College, Hanover, New Hampshire. Courtesy of Wikimedia Commons.*

The governor met with his council on July 18, 1775. He announced to them that "the People of the County of Bladen were pursuing the example of the People of Mecklenburg, whose treasonable proceedings he had communicated to the Council at the last meeting," and that "he desired the advice of the Council on the measures expedient to be taken to counteract such unwarrantable and dangerous extravagancies." He also stated that one of the Council members "is of the opinion that His Excellency should take every lawful measure in his power to suppress the unnatural rebellion now fomenting in Mecklenburgh."

Martin was right that the rebellion in Mecklenburg was spreading to other parts of North Carolina. On June 20, fifty residents of Cumberland County signed the "Liberty Point Resolves," which protested the actions of Great Britain in the Battles of Lexington and Concord and the arbitrary impositions imposed by them since the battles. It also vowed that, if necessary, they would "go forth and be ready to sacrifice our lives and fortunes to secure her [the colonies] freedom and safety." Forty-nine inhabitants of Tryon County signed the August 14 "Tryon Resolves," which called for a redress of wrongs inflicted on the colonies from the British Parliament and the Crown. They also formed a county militia in preparation for a British retaliation against American resistance. Committees from the counties of New Hanover, Brunswick, Bladen, Duplin and Onslow sent an angry response to Governor Martin's proclamation of June 16, in which, according to their letter, the governor:

> *Endeavored to persuade, seduce, and intimidate the good people of the province, from taking measures to preserve those rights, and that liberty, to which, as subjects of a British King they have the most undoubted claim, without which therefore, it is the duty they owe to themselves, their Country, and posterity, by every effort, and at every risk, to maintain, support, and defend against any invasion or encroachment whatsoever.*

The letter then explained how they viewed Governor Martin:

> *We then, the Committees of the counties of New Hanover, Brunswick, Bladen, Duplin and Onslow, in order to prevent the pernicious influence of the said Proclamation, do, unanimously, resolve, that in our opinion, his excellency Josiah Martin, Esq.; hath by the said Proclamation, and by the whole tenor of his conduct, since the unhappy dispute between Great Britain and the colonies, discovered himself to be an enemy to the happiness of this colony in particular, and to the freedom, rights, and privileges of America in general.*

The spreading rebellion throughout the province could be attributed to Reverend Alexander Craighead for having planted the seeds of rebellion starting seventeen years earlier when he began to preach in and around Mecklenburg County.

Not only was the rebellion in Mecklenburg County catching fire in the rest of the province, but word of the Mecklenburg Resolves was also being read in the North. The articles of the Resolves that appeared in the North and South Carolina newspapers from June 13 through June 23 were reprinted in the *New York Journal* on June 29, in the *Massachusetts Spy* on July 12 and in several other newspapers in the northern colonies about the same time. The *Massachusetts Spy* was particularly well suited for an article about a county in North Carolina rebelling against Great Britain and declaring the laws of the king of England and Parliament null and void. Below the newspaper's title were printed the words "Do thou Great Liberty inspire our Souls—And make our Lives in Thy Possession happy—Or, our Deaths glorious in Thy just Defence [*sic*]. Join or Die." The newspaper had been forced to move out of Boston to the safer Worcester, Massachusetts, by the British authorities because of its obvious revolutionary position. The rebellious actions in Mecklenburg and North Carolina were encouraging the revolutionaries in the North, leading them toward independence.

In July 1775, Governor Martin wrote to General Thomas Gage of the British army requesting a supply of arms and ammunition. In his letter, he confided to the general about his plans to arm slaves against the rebels in the province. The letter was intercepted, and John Ashe, an officer in the North Carolina Militia and a member of the Provincial Congress, marched with five hundred men to Fort Johnston, near present-day Wilmington, where the governor had his office. The men forced Martin to flee to the sloop-of-war *Cruiser* on July 20 and demolished the fort. Because the governor had fled, the Provincial Congress authorized its own North Carolina currency in 1775, which was printed by James Davis of New Bern, who had become the first printer in North Carolina in 1749.

Dr. Ephraim Brevard, an elder in the Hopewell church and a former parishioner of Reverend Craighead, wrote to four of his good friends on September 1, 1775. The recipients of the letter were Thomas Polk; Waightstill Avery; John Phifer, an elder at the Rocky River church; and John McKnitt Alexander, secretary of the convention and an elder at the Hopewell church. They were Mecklenburg's delegates to the Provincial Congress that was meeting in Hillsborough. The letter was titled "Instructions for the delegates of Mecklenburg County, proposed to the consideration of the county," and read as follows:

> *1st. You are instructed to vote that the late Province of North Carolina is, and of right ought to be, a free and independent State; is vested with the powers of Legislation, capable of making laws to regulate all the internal police, subject only in its internal connections and foreign commerce, to a negative of a continental Senate.*
>
> *2d. You are instructed to vote for the execution of a civil government under the authority of the people, for the future security of all the rights, privileges, and prerogatives of the State, and the private, natural and unalienable rights of the constituting members thereof, either as men or Christians. If this should not be confirmed in Congress, or Convention,—protest.*
>
> *3d. You are instructed to vote that an equal representation be established, and that the qualifications required to enable any person or persons to have a voice in legislation may not be screwed too high, but that every freeman, who shall be called upon to support government, either in person or property, may be admitted thereto. If this should not be confirmed,—protest and remonstrate.*
>
> *In the fourth and fifth, aristocratic honors are to be done way with, and the right of property confirmed. In the sixth, deputies to the Continental*

Continental Congress at Philadelphia. *Painting by Robert Edge Pine, 1784–1788, Independence Hall, Philadelphia. Courtesy of Wikimedia Commons.*

Congress are to be appointed by the supreme legislative body. In the seventh, the election of all officers, civil and military, is to be confirmed by the people at large. In the eighth, no public officer should be a representative in Congress or Convention. In the ninth, tenth, and eleventh, the expenditure of public money is to be brought more within the power of the people. In the thirteenth, the Christian religion is to be established by the State to the exclusion of the false religions, whether pagan or papal.

14th. You are instructed to oppose to the utmost, any particular church or set of clergymen being invested with power to decree rites and ceremonies, and to decide in controversies of faith, to be submitted to under the influence of penal laws. You are also to oppose the establishment of any mode of worship to be supported to the oppression of the rights of conscience, together with the destruction of private property. You are to understand that under the modes of worship are comprehended the different forms of swearing by law required. You are, moreover, to oppose the establishing an ecclesiastical supremacy in the sovereign authority of the State. You are to oppose the toleration of popish idolatrous worship. If this should not be confirmed,—protest and remonstrate.

> *In the fourteenth, four-fifths of the Provincial Congress is to be considered a majority, and in the sixteenth, give your voice for all motions and bills in Congress or Convention that serve the public good.*
>
> *17th. Gentlemen, the foregoing instructions you are not only to look upon as instructions, but as charges, to which you are desired to take special heed, as the ground of your conduct as our Representatives; and we expect you will exert yourselves to the utmost of your ability to obtain the purposes given you in charge; and wherein you fail, either in obtaining or opposing, you are hereby ordered to enter your protest against the vote of Congress or Convention, as is pointed out to you in the above instructions.*

The thirteenth and fourteenth instructions present a new concept of religious liberty among Protestant denominations, but since the instructions were written by a Scotch-Irish Presbyterian, they exclude the Roman Catholic religion within that concept of religious liberty.

The movement of North Carolina toward independence reached an important milestone on April 12, 1776, when the eighty-three delegates to the Provincial Congress, which included John McKnitt Alexander, John Philfer, Thomas Polk and Waightstill Avery, agreed to the following resolution:

> *Resolved, that the delegates for this Colony in the Continental Congress be empowered to concur with the delegates of the other Colonies in declaring independence, and forming foreign alliances, reserving to this Colony the sole and exclusive right of forming a constitution and laws for this Colony, and of appointing delegates from time to time (under the direction of a general representative thereof), to meet the delegates of other Colonies.*

The resolution became known as the Halifax Resolves, and with its enactment, North Carolina became the first colony to instruct its delegates to the Continental Congress in Philadelphia to agree to a national declaration of independence.

The preachings of Reverend Alexander Craighead on the importance of being independent from England and resistance to colonial authorities aroused his parishioners to rebellious acts, including the War of Sugar Creek, the actions of the Mecklenburg Black Boys in blowing up the British ammunition wagon train near Concord and the Mecklenburg Declaration of Independence and Mecklenburg Resolves. These actions had emboldened other North Carolina citizens to resist colonial authorities in the Hillsborough disturbances; the Battle of Alamance, the country's first

Revolutionary War battle; the resistance of the North Carolina Assembly to Governor Josiah Martin; the formation of the North Carolina Provincial Congress; the resolves passed by other counties; the destruction of Fort Johnston, forcing Martin to govern from a ship; and the adoption of the Halifax Resolves by the Provincial Congress. The reports of these actions spread to other colonies through newspaper articles and word of mouth, creating more discussions and a change of thinking toward the need for independence from England throughout the country.

Chapter 8

MECKLENBURG'S ROLE IN THE REVOLUTIONARY WAR

In 1775, 70 percent of the residents of Mecklenburg County in North Carolina had been parishioners in the seven churches pastored by Reverend Alexander Craighead. He also served as a missionary minister to outlying churches, such as Unity Presbyterian Church near Beattie's Ford on the Catawba River north of present-day Charlotte and groups in the process of becoming churches, such as the Presbyterian gathering at Clear Creek, which became the Philadelphia Presbyterian Church in 1770. Craighead advocated independence from Great Britain with fiery sermons and also preached that his parishioners should resist government authorities, on both the state and county levels. He argued that the governor and his council were merely extensions of the Crown because they were appointed by the king's officials. Craighead felt that the state legislature, which did not fairly represent the North Carolina backcountry, imposed unfair burdens on Presbyterians with the Marriage Act, which allowed them to be married only by Anglican ministers, and the Vestry Act, which forced Presbyterians to pay taxes to support the Anglican Church. The legislature had also refused to enact laws preventing county officials from charging excessive land taxes, much of which the officials pocketed for themselves. The citizens of Mecklenburg understood Reverend Craighead's message, and this was demonstrated when they rebelled against the government in the War of Sugar Creek, the destruction of a British ammunition wagon train by the Mecklenburg Black Boys, their participation in the Battle of Alamance and their signing the Mecklenburg Declaration of Independence and Resolves. The fighting of

Mecklenburg citizens in the Revolutionary War was another example of doing what their beloved minister told them to do. When the Revolutionary War began, Mecklenburg County represented less than 3 percent of the population of North Carolina, but the county provided about 25 percent of the soldiers from the colony. This was determined by projecting the total number of soldiers from Mecklenburg County from the number of known Mecklenburg officers based on the ratio of officers to all soldiers for North Carolina. The actual names of officers for Mecklenburg were determined much more readily than the names of the Mecklenburg soldiers without rank. The large number of Revolutionary soldiers from Mecklenburg County is just another testament to the strength of Reverend Craighead's preaching in support of independence from England. This book's appendix has a listing of the known 507 Revolutionary War soldiers from Mecklenburg County and shows which Reverend Craighead church the soldiers attended, if that information is available. It is likely that about 70 percent of Mecklenburg's soldiers were parishioners of Reverend Craighead. For the Mecklenburg officers, the appendix also shows the battles in which they were wounded, captured or killed.

Following are descriptions of the Revolutionary War battles the Mecklenburg soldiers fought in, as well as the names of the Mecklenburg officers who led them in those battles. The Mecklenburg officers and soldiers were inspired by the words of Reverend Craighead as they fought in those battles, and together they played an important role in the Revolutionary War. The Scotch-Irish were natural fighters. Their history, especially that of the lowland Scots, who accounted for most of the immigration to Ireland and to America, included over one thousand years of fighting the English. They hated the English, whom they continued to battle after moving to Ireland. They also fought the Irish during their years in Ulster. When they migrated to America, it was the Scotch-Irish, for the most part, who fought the Indians, since they lived on the frontiers. Other colonists induced the Scotch-Irish to come to America to be a buffer against the Indians because of their known fighting skills. General Robert E. Lee knew firsthand what great fighters the Scotch-Irish were from his Civil War experience. When he was asked the question, "What race of people do you believe make the best soldiers?" His answer was, "The Scots who came to this country by way of Ireland. Because they have all the dash of the Irish in taking up a position and all the stubbornness of the Scots in holding it." It's not surprising that although the Scotch-Irish accounted for only 9.8 percent of the white population in the colonies in 1775, it is estimated that they accounted for at least 40 percent of the American soldiers in the Revolutionary War. Some estimates are over 50 percent. Leaders in England, America and others thought of the Revolutionary War as being driven by the Scotch-Irish Presbyterians. King George III described the Revolution as "a Presbyterian war," and a member of the British Parliament, Horace Walpole, the Earl of Orford, remarked in one of the sessions, "There is no use crying about it. Cousin America has run off with a Presbyterian parson." An agent of Lord Dartmouth, the colonial secretary, wrote from New York in 1776, "Presbyterianism is really at the Bottom of the whole Conspiracy, has supplied it with Vigour [*sic*], and will never rest, till something is decided upon." John D. Sergeant, a New Jersey representative to the Continental Congress, declared that the Scotch-Irish were the main pillar of the Revolution. And a captain in the thirty-thousand-man German mercenary army hired by England to fight in the war wrote in 1778, "Call this war by whatever name you may, only call it not an American rebellion; it is nothing more or less than a Scotch-Irish rebellion."

Even before the United States Declaration of Independence was signed, the Mecklenburg County Regiment of Militia led by three signers of the Mecklenburg Declaration—Colonel Thomas Polk; Major John Phifer, an elder in the Rocky River church; and Second Major John Davidson, a member of the Hopewell church—fought in the Snow Campaign, which started near Ninety Six, South Carolina, on December 23, 1775. The six companies in the regiment were led by Mecklenburg officers Captain Robert Irwin, a Mecklenburg Declaration signer and a member of the Steele Creek church; Captain James Jack, the carrier of the Mecklenburg papers to the Continental Congress in Philadelphia and an elder of the Providence church; Captain James Alexander, a member of the Sugaw Creek church; Captain William Alexander, a member of the Sugaw Creek church; Captain James Harris, a Mecklenburg Declaration signer and a member of the Philadelphia Presbyterian Church, which was called the Presbyterian gathering at Clear Creek before 1770; Captain James Houston, a member of the Centre church; Captain John Barringer; Captain Cromisle; Captain Isaac Houston; Captain Caleb Phifer; Captain Moses Shelby; and Captain Thomas Shelby. William Polk, son of Colonel Thomas Polk, was a soldier in his father's regiment. They were part of an army of three thousand militia under the command of Colonel Richard Richardson, who marched against Scovelite Loyalist recruiting centers in South Carolina from present-day Greenville southeast to present-day Lexington. They were called Scovelites after a Tory leader named Joseph Scoffel, who was active in the Loyalist cause from an early period. It was known as the Snow Campaign because of the unusual two feet of snowfall in the later stages of the campaign. The peak size of the Loyalist force was about four hundred men. The campaign was successful. It wiped out the British centers and frustrated their attempts to organize, basically eliminating Loyalist activity in the backcountry area. Only one Patriot soldier was wounded, while Loyalists had 6 men killed and 130 captured. Most of the prisoners were released "as a conciliatory gesture to the backcountry friends." Soon after the Snow Campaign, several young women in Mecklenburg County announced they would date only young men who had fought in the Snow Campaign. The *South Carolina and American General Gazette* reported in the February 1776 issue, "The young ladies of the best families of Mecklenburg County, North Carolina, have entered into a voluntary association that they will not receive addresses of any young gentlemen of that place, except the brave volunteers who served in the expedition to South Carolina, and assisted in subduing the Scovelite insurgents."

Two months later, Colonel Polk marched his Mecklenburg County Regiment of Militia to Cross Creek, near present-day Fayetteville, North Carolina, to suppress a Tory uprising, arriving there on February 22, 1776. Serving under Polk were Mecklenburg officers Lieutenant Colonel Adam

Plaque to signers of the Mecklenburg Declaration. *Photo by author.*

Alexander, a Mecklenburg Declaration signer and an elder in the Rocky River church, and Major John Phifer. Five companies in the regiment were led by signers of the Mecklenburg Declaration: Captain John McKnitt Alexander, Captain Ephraim Brevard and Captain Matthew McClure, all elders in the Hopewell church; Captain Robert Irwin, a member of the Steele Creek church; and Captain John Davidson, a Mecklenburg Declaration signer and a member of the Hopewell church. The expedition was successful in eliminating Loyalist recruiting in the area.

Colonel Polk and the regiment marched from Cross Creek on to Moore's Creek, North Carolina, which was twenty miles north of Wilmington. They were joined en route by six more companies led by Mecklenburg officers Captain James Alexander, a member of the Steele Creek church; Captain James Barns; Captain John McRee, a member of the Steele Creek church; Captain Samuel Patton; Captain Caleb Phifer; and Captain Robert Smith. The Patriot militia force now had a total of 1,000 men, and the Loyalist militia was 1,500 strong. The Loyalists had only five hundred firearms and were mostly armed with broadswords and pikes. The Loyalists expected to find only a small Patriot force, so on February 27, 1776, 80 men armed with broadswords charged across the Moore's Creek Bridge, shouting, "King George and broadswords!" only to be met with severe Patriot fire at point-blank range coming from the adjoining woods. The attacking group was mowed down in minutes, with no one left standing on the bridge. Most of the Loyalists quickly fled or surrendered. In the Battle of Moore's Creek, only 1 Patriot was killed and 1 wounded, while the Loyalists had 20 killed or wounded and 850 captured. The Patriots also captured wagons, weapons and British sterling worth $1 million in today's market. The victory ended British governmental authority in North Carolina and prevented organized Loyalist activity in the area for several years. It also inspired the North Carolina Provincial Congress to pass the Halifax Resolves with instructions to the delegates to the Continental Congress in Philadelphia to vote for independence from Great Britain.

The North Carolina Provincial Congress established six Continental army regiments on April 9, 1776. Colonel Thomas Polk, a Mecklenburg Declaration signer, was made commander of the Fourth North Carolina Regiment with Major William Lee Davidson third in command. Major Davidson lived on a plantation in the northernmost part of Mecklenburg County, attended Reverend Craighead's Sugaw Creek Academy and later Liberty Hall Academy and was a member of the Centre church. Later in the war, he was promoted to brigadier general. Davidson College and the town of Davidson were later named after him, and most of the land for the college came from his estate. Major William Lee Davidson was a second cousin, once removed, of Captain John Davidson, a Mecklenburg Declaration signer. The regiment marched toward Charleston, South Carolina, in June 1776 to defend the city against an invasion by a British fleet but was ordered back to North Carolina to guard the coast against British raids. In May 1777, the regiment, along with the other eight North Carolina regiments, marched to Philadelphia to join General George Washington's army. Along the way, the troops stopped in Alexandria, Virginia, to be inoculated for smallpox, which provided a lifetime immunity.

On September 11, 1777, General Washington's army of 14,600 men met the British-Hessian army of 15,500 near Chadd's Ford on Brandywine Creek in Pennsylvania, about twenty miles west of Philadelphia. North Carolina sent nine regiments to the North to be part of Washington's army, as well as three companies of dragoons (mounted troops) and two artillery companies. There were several Mecklenburg officers in those North Carolina units. Colonel Thomas Polk led the Fourth North Carolina Regiment with Major William Lee Davidson, a member of the Centre church, and First Lieutenant Alexander Brevard within his command group. Alexander was a brother of Dr. Ephraim Brevard, a signer of the Mecklenburg Declaration and an elder in the Hopewell church. Alexander and Ephraim had five other brothers who fought in the Revolutionary War, all sons of the widow Jane McWhorter Brevard, who was a member of the Centre church. Later in the war, British lieutenant general Charles Cornwallis ordered that her house be burned down because she had so many sons fighting against the British. Other Mecklenburg officers were Captain John Nelson and Captain James Wilson in the Fourth; Lieutenant Colonel Davis and Major John Walker in the First North Carolina Regiment; Captain John Martin, a member of the Rocky River church, in the Second North Carolina Regiment; Lieutenant Colonel William Lee Davidson, a member of the Centre church, in the Fifth North Carolina Regiment; Captain John Griffith McRee, a member of the Steel Creek church; Captain Thomas White, a member of the Rocky River church, and Captain Daniel Williams in the Sixth North Carolina Regiment; Major William Polk, son of Colonel Thomas Polk, and Captain James Hall in the Ninth North Carolina Regiment; Captain James Wilkins, a member of the Steele Creek church, in the Tenth North Carolina Regiment; Captain Samuel Ashe Jr. leading the First Company of North Carolina Light Dragoons; and Captain Martin Phifer leading the Second Company of North Carolina Light Dragoons. At Brandywine Creek, the

Battle of Brandywine Creek. *Painting by Howard Pyle, 1906, Brandywine River Museum. Courtesy of Wikimedia Commons.*

British forces were led by General William Howe, and because of poor scouting by the Patriots, a column of the British army was able to reach the rear of Washington's army's right flank. The British forces then were able to break through both the right and left flanks of the Americans, and the Patriots went into retreat. In the Battle of Brandywine Creek, Washington's army suffered 300 killed, 600 wounded and 400 captured, while the British army had 93 killed, 488 wounded and 6 missing. Washington's army retreated back to Philadelphia.

As the British forces advanced toward Philadelphia, the Patriots' command headquarters, General Washington ordered Colonel Thomas Polk to lead a detachment of 200 Mecklenburg Continental soldiers with numerous wagons to remove twenty-three large brass bells out of Philadelphia, including the Pennsylvania State House Bell, which became known as the Liberty Bell in the 1830s. The bells were removed to prevent the British from melting down the bells for cannonballs. The State House Bell had been rung, along with the other Philadelphia bells, when the United States Declaration of Independence was read on July 8, 1776. The Liberty Bell was initially cracked when it was first rung in 1752 and was recast twice. The large crack presently on the bell occurred when it was rung in the early nineteenth century. Colonel Polk delivered all the bells to Bethlehem, Pennsylvania, and then led the men and wagons back to Philadelphia. Washington's army left Philadelphia, and on September 26, the British occupied the city, an occupation that would last until June 1778. British general William Howe left 3,462 men in Philadelphia to defend the city and moved 9,728 men to Germantown, Pennsylvania, five miles north of Philadelphia.

General Washington believed that with the British forces divided, it was an opportunity to attack them at Germantown before the beginning of winter. Washington's army still included all the North Carolina units with the same Mecklenburg officers who fought in the Battle of Brandywine Creek. After nightfall on October 3, 1777, the American forces marched in complete darkness from the north of the town. The men put white pieces of paper on their hats to show they were Patriots. Because of the darkness, their progress was slow. At dawn, they were far short of their planned attack positions, and they forfeited the intent of surprise. Washington's army made many furious attacks, but they were continuously beaten back and suffered heavy casualties. Washington was finally forced to retreat. The British army pursued them for about five miles and broke off. It was a British victory. In the Battle of Germantown, Patriot forces had 152 killed, 521 wounded and 438 captured. Among the wounded were Colonel

Right: Liberty Bell. *Photo by Tony Fischer. Courtesy of Wikimedia Commons.*

Below: Map of the Battle of Germantown. *Spenser Bonsall Map, 1877. Courtesy of Wikimedia Commons.*

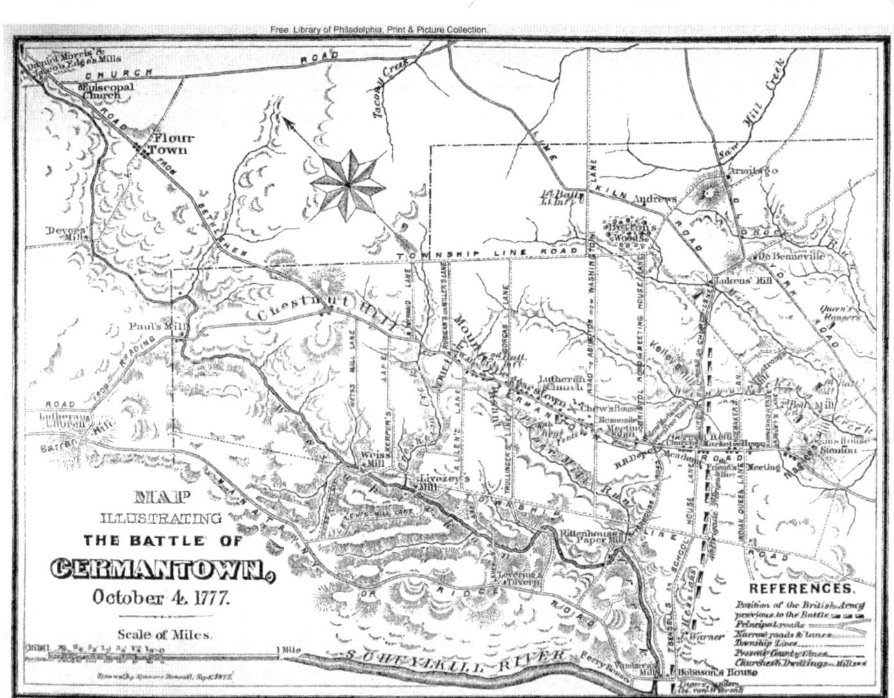

Thomas Polk and his son Major William Polk, who was badly wounded in the jaw. The Patriots' Brigadier General Francis Nash had his left leg taken off by a cannonball and died four days later. The British forces had 71 killed, 448 wounded and 14 missing.

Winter was setting in, and General Washington made the decision to camp at Valley Forge, Pennsylvania, about twenty-five miles northwest of Philadelphia. The town was named for an iron forge on Valley Creek. The 12,000 men included the nine North Carolina regiments and the dragoon and artillery companies with the same Mecklenburg officers, except that Major William Lee Davidson had been promoted to lieutenant colonel and given the command of the Fifth North Carolina Regiment. They were all poorly fed and tired from lengthy marches. Only about one-third of the men had shoes, and their feet were bloody from all the marching. One thousand huts were made within six weeks, but the men suffered from the wet conditions of the freezing and melting snow. Some had to live on "fire cake," a tasteless mixture of heated flour and water, but most got fresh-baked bread daily. There were few blankets, and the men wore tattered clothing. Hundreds of horses either starved to death or died of exhaustion. At one point, 4,000 men were listed as unfit for duty. Washington repeatedly asked the Continental Congress for relief, but it was unable to provide it. According to Washington, the North Carolina regiments were more sickly than the other colonies' regiments because of the lack of provisions and clothing, being so far from home. They also suffered heavier losses, with 204 deaths out of 1,072 men, and fewer than half their soldiers were fit for duty at any one time. About 500 women, mostly relatives of the men, helped by washing laundry, mending uniforms and nursing the sick. With all the suffering, only "dozens" of the soldiers deserted, and it was reported that all the Scotch-Irish men remained in camp. There were forty-two court-martials, and most of those trials were for desertion or attempted desertion. About 2,500 men died at Valley Forge from typhoid, jaundice, dysentery and pneumonia. In the spring of 1778, the North Carolina regiments were so depleted that Washington ordered that the Fourth, Fifth and Sixth Regiments be absorbed by the First, Second and Third Regiments. The Seventh, Eighth and Ninth Regiments were disbanded on May 27, 1778. Colonel Thomas Polk and other officers were sent back to North Carolina to recruit replacements and lead the new regiments. It was learned that the British army had left Philadelphia in June 1778 and was heading to New York. On June 19, 1778, Washington's army left Valley Forge in pursuit of the British. The Patriots considered Valley Forge a victory.

Washington & Lafayette at Valley Forge. *Engraving by H.B. Hall after painting by Alonzo Chappel, 1857. Courtesy of Wikimedia Commons.*

The first major engagement after the winter at Valley Forge and the last battle in the North before the British soldiers shifted their attention to the South was the Battle of Monmouth, New Jersey, on June 28, 1778. General George Washington moved his 12,000 Continental troops across the Delaware River with the aim of attacking General Henry Clinton as he marched his 11,000 British troops from Philadelphia to New York. Washington's North Carolina units included a number of Mecklenburg officers. The newly promoted Lieutenant Colonel William Lee Davidson, a member of the Centre church, now led the Third North Carolina Regiment, which included the old Fifth. Major John Nelson was a leader of the First North Carolina Regiment with Captain John Griffith McRee, a member of the Steele Creek church, the head of one of its companies; Captain Samuel Ashe Jr. was head of the First Company of North Carolina Light Dragoons; Captain Martin Phifer was head of the Second Company of North Carolina Light Dragoons; and Captain John Brown, a member of the Steele Creek church, was head of the Third Company of North Carolina Light Dragoons. Captain James Jack, who carried the Mecklenburg Declaration to Philadelphia and was an elder in the Providence church, led a company of the North Carolina Militia.

Washington sent Major General Charles Lee with 5,000 men to harass Clinton's rear guard near the Monmouth Courthouse, but Lee used his men in a piecemeal fashion and was outflanked and forced to retreat. Washington came upon the retreating troops, sharply rebuked Lee and rallied the troops. Repeated British advances were beaten off, and the fighting stopped, with each side claiming victory. In the Battle of Monmouth, the official report of the Continental army was 65 killed, 37 dead from heat-stroke, 160 wounded and 95 missing, and that of the British was 65 killed, 59 dead from heat-stroke, 170 wounded, 50 captured and 14 missing. These numbers were conservative, and it's likely the losses for the Patriots were 500 to 600 men and 1,100 for the British.

In 1779, Charleston, South Carolina, was the site of the Continental army's southern command, led by General Benjamin Lincoln. Mecklenburg officers included Colonel John Allison of the North Carolina Militia; Captain James Campbell, leader of a company in the Fifth North Carolina Regiment; Captain William Ganns, leader of a company in the Sixth North Carolina Regiment; and Captain James White, leader of a company in the Sixth South Carolina Regiment. James White was one of the Mecklenburg Black Boys and a member of the Rocky River church. The Mecklenburg officers

Washington at the Battle of Monmouth. *Painting by unknown artist, 1850, National Archives and Records Administration, College Park, Maryland. Courtesy of Wikimedia Commons.*

also included Captain William Richardson Davie, leader of a company in the North Carolina Light Dragoons. William Richardson Davie had a close connection to Reverend Alexander Craighead. When Davie was nine years old, his family moved to Waxham in Mecklenburg County to be near his maternal uncle Reverend William Richardson, after whom Davie was named. Reverend Richardson had married Reverend Craighead's daughter Agnes Nancy, and Waxham was only ten miles from Reverend Craighead's Providence church. It is likely that Davie heard Reverend Craighead preach about independence from England or at least knew well Reverend Craighead's convictions. When Reverend Richardson died, Davie inherited 150 acres of land and his large library, since his uncle had no children of his own. Davie went on to study at Liberty Hall Academy, the former Queens College, and the College of New Jersey, which became Princeton University. He eventually became the tenth governor of North Carolina in 1798 and one of the founders of the University of North Carolina. In mid-April, General Lincoln decided the troops were strong enough to move against British-held Savannah, but when British general Augustine Prevoust found out the Americans were marching toward Savannah, he decided to take 2,500 men and march to Charleston. Learning this, General Lincoln turned around his army of 1,500 men and headed back to Charleston. Provoust left 900 men under Lieutenant Colonel John Maitland at Stono Ferry, which was on the south side of the bay into Charleston just north of John's Island, and headed back to Savannah with the rest of the men. The Patriots attacked the British position at Stono Ferry on June 20, 1779, with small arms and cannon fire for an hour, killing most of the Highlanders in two companies. The Hessians began to produce heavy casualties among the Patriots, and General Lincoln ordered a retreat. It was a British victory. In the Battle of Stono Ferry, the Americans had 34 killed, 113 wounded and 155 missing. Hugh Jackson, the brother of future president Andrew Jackson, died from heat exhaustion, and Captain William Richardson Davie suffered a severe wound in his thigh, fell from his horse and was almost captured. Colonel John Allison was wounded, and Captain James Campbell was wounded and captured. He was exchanged for British prisoners on June 14, 1781. In the Battle of Stono Ferry, the British had 26 killed, 93 wounded and 1 missing. Lieutenant Colonel Maitland moved the remaining British troops to Beaufort, South Carolina, on June 23.

The siege of Charleston began on March 29, 1780, with 13,500 British infantrymen, marines, sailors and militia and ninety ships commanded by Major General Henry Clinton. The Patriots were led by Major General

Benjamin Lincoln and included a total army of 5,466 infantrymen and militia. Mecklenburg officers included First Lieutenant Robert Hays; Surgeon Ephraim Brevard, a signer of the Mecklenburg Declaration and an elder at the Hopewell church, and Surgeon William McClure in the North Carolina First Regiment of Militia; Lieutenant William Walker in the North Carolina Second Regiment of Militia; and Lieutenant Thomas Allen, Captain Jacob Collins and Captain Simmerson in the North Carolina Third Regiment of Militia. Major General Clinton marched on Charleston across James Island. The sides exchanged artillery fire. Clinton approached slowly and steadily with the British digging siege trenches closer and closer to the wall of the city. By the beginning of May, the British were within a few feet of the Patriots' lines, and their artillery fire was causing heavy casualties among the Americans and setting houses on fire in the city. The siege cut off the city from any relief, and General Lincoln was forced to surrender after six weeks on May 12, 1780. In the siege of Charleston, American casualties were 76 killed and 182 wounded, while British losses were 92 killed and 148 wounded. The total number of Patriots captured was 5,266, including General Lincoln and all 7 of the Mecklenburg officers. First Lieutenant Thomas Allen died in prison on August 26, 1780, Major John Nelson was exchanged for British prisoners in March 1781 and the other 5 officers were exchanged for British prisoners on June 14, 1781. Dr. Ephraim Brevard became very ill as a prisoner, and he traveled back to Charlotte, still very weak, and stayed at the home of his friend and fellow Mecklenburg Declaration signer John McKnitt Alexander. He never recovered and died there in 1781. The British controlled Charleston until December 14, 1782.

In June 1780, Patriot general Griffith Rutherford, encamped near Charlotte, North Carolina, learned that Loyalists were gathering near Ramsour's Mill, owned by Jacob Ramsour, about twenty-five miles northwest of Charlotte, near present-day Lincolnton. He sent a message to Colonel Francis Locke and other militia leaders to call up their men. Locke gathered a total of 400 men, including the Mecklenburg County Regiment of Militia detachment led by Major James Harris, a Mecklenburg Declaration signer and a member of the Philadelphia Presbyterian Church, and Major Robert Wilson, a member of the Hopewell church. The regiment included thirteen companies led by Mecklenburg officers Captain Ezra Alexander, a signer of the Mecklenburg Declaration; Captain William Alexander, a member of the Sugaw Creek church; Captain Samuel Givens; Captain James Houston, a member of the Centre church; Captain James Huggins; Captain

Patrick Knox; Captain James Ligert; Captain Samuel Martin; Captain John McFalls; Captain David Reed; Captain George Reed; Captain William Smith, a member of the Providence church; and Captain John Sterns. The Rowan County Second Regiment of Militia was led by Mecklenburg officer Lieutenant Colonel Frederick Hambright. Even though Colonel Locke learned that the British had 1,300 men, more than three times his troop size, he decided to attack the British on June 20 on land owned by Christian Reinhardt. He made an initial cavalry charge, and his infantry was able to break through the Loyalist flank, and the Patriots took control of a ridge. Locke was unable to reform his line on the ridge, so he ordered a retreat, but Captain John Dickey disobeyed his order and, with a good position on the ridge and the marksmanship of his company's men, gave a victory to the Patriots. General Rutherford, with Colonel William Lee Davidson, arrived too late to help, but by then aid was no longer needed. In the Battle of Ramsour's Mill, about 50 to 70 men on each side were killed, including Captain Patrick Knox, and about 100 wounded, including Captain James Houston and Captain George Reed, but the American victory helped raise the morale of the Patriots and so demoralized the Loyalists that they never organized in that area again.

Christian Reinhardt log cabin at Ramsour's Mill Battle Site. *Photo by author.*

Colonel William Lee Davidson and his regiment were in the process of pursuing Loyalists when he learned on July 21, 1780, that several hundred Loyalists were gathering at Colson's Mill near present-day Norwood, North Carolina, about forty miles east of Charlotte. Included in Davidson's Mecklenburg County Regiment of Militia detachment were 250 Patriots in eight companies led by Mecklenburg officers Captain Ezra Alexander, a Mecklenburg Declaration signer; Captain Alexander Brevard, brother of Dr. Ephraim Brevard, a Mecklenburg Declaration signer and an elder in the Hopewell church; Captain James Byers, a member of the Centre church; Captain Samuel Givens; Captain Charles Polk, brother of Colonel Thomas Polk; Captain Thomas Ray; Captain Richard Springs; and Captain Zaccheus Wilson, a Mecklenburg Declaration signer and an elder in the Steele Creek church. Davidson attempted to surprise the 400 Loyalists at the farm and surrounded it, but they realized the Patriots' presence and began firing. Davidson was the only man in uniform, so he became a target and was severely shot in the stomach. His men did not falter when he went down, and their fighting sent the Loyalists fleeing. In the Battle of Colson's Mill, 3 Loyalists were killed and 10 were taken prisoner. The Patriots had 2 men wounded, including Colonel Davidson, who spent two months recovering.

During 1779 and early 1780, the British were able to take control of South Carolina and Georgia. They set up outposts to recruit Loyalists and suppress Patriot dissent. One outpost was in Rocky Mount, South Carolina, about forty miles south of Charlotte, near present-day Great Falls. Since there was no Patriot Continental army command structure in the South, Brigadier General Thomas Sumter was raising a militia force and had about three hundred men in late July 1780. Sumter decided to attack the outpost at Rocky Mount on July 31, 1780, sending Mecklenburg's Major William Richardson Davie and his company of dragoons to another outpost as a diversionary strategy. Sumter's forces included a Mecklenburg County Militia detachment led by Mecklenburg officers Colonel Robert Irwin and Lieutenant Colonel William Polk, son of Colonel Thomas Polk. The five companies in the detachment were led by Mecklenburg officers Captain William Alexander, a member of the Sugaw Creek church; Captain William Hutchinson; Captain James Nathaniel Martin, a member of the Rocky River church; Captain George Reed; and Captain Richard Springs. Sumter learned through a spy that the outpost's defenses, with about six hundred men, were susceptible to small arms fire, which would aid the Patriots since they had no field artillery. The spy was likely a double agent because when the Patriots attacked the defenses, Sumter realized that the defenses had been strengthened, and the Americans were unable to penetrate the structure. They attempted to burn down the outpost, but a heavy rain put out the fire and ended the battle. In the Battle of Rocky Mount, the Patriots had twelve men killed or wounded, and the Loyalists had twenty killed or wounded. The battle was considered a British victory because the Patriots were unable to penetrate the outpost.

Just six days later and thirteen miles to the east, Brigadier General Thomas Sumter decided to attack the British outpost at Hanging Rock on the Catawba River in South Carolina on August 6, 1780. This time he had a total of 800 Patriot militiamen, who included the Mecklenburg County Militia Regiment led by Mecklenburg officers Colonel Robert Irwin, Lieutenant Colonel John William Hagan and Major John Davidson, a Mecklenburg Declaration signer and a member of the Hopewell church. The regiment consisted of 200 men in thirteen companies led by Mecklenburg officers Captain Robert Craighead, son of Reverend Alexander Craighead; Captain William Alexander, a member of the Sugaw Creek church; Captain John Brownfield; Captain James Knox, a member of the Hopewell church; Captain James Nathaniel Martin, a member of the Poplar Tent church; Captain Charles McKee; Captain Robert McKnight; Captain Francis Miller; Captain Luke Petty; Captain David Reed; Captain George Reed; Captain Richard Springs; and Captain John Sterns. Sumter's army also included another Mecklenburg County Regiment, an Independent Corps of Light Horse led by Major William Richardson Davie with eight companies led by Mecklenburg officer Captain Thomas Alexander, a member of the Sugaw Creek church; Captain Samuel Flanagan; Captain John Foster; Captain Meshack Gentry; Captain John Harris, a member of the Steele Creek church; Captain John Locke; Captain Nathaniel Marshall Martin; and Captain James Wiley. Ensign James McClure, a member of the Steele Creek church, was an officer in the North Carolina Militia, and David Flenniker, a brother of John Flenniker, a signer of the Mecklenburg Declaration and a member of the Providence church, was a soldier in one of the units. The outpost was well fortified with 1,400 Loyalist provincial troops and militia led by Major John Carden. Major Davie had preceded Sumter to Hanging Rock and had attacked a fortified house outside the outpost, capturing sixty horses and inflicting a few casualties on the British. Initial attacks by Sumter on the outpost caused heavy casualties against the Loyalists. The battle lasted for three hours without ceasing, and at the peak of the battle, Loyalist major Carden had become fearful and turned his command over to a junior officer, which seemed to turn the battle to the favor of the Americans, who gained victory when the Loyalists surrendered. In the Battle of Hanging Rock, the British had 192 soldiers killed or wounded, and the Patriots had 12 killed and 41 wounded. Captain Robert Craighead was wounded and saved by a Catawba Indian, who was fighting on the side of the Americans. Captain Luke Perry was wounded, and his arm was shot off. Captain George Reed was wounded and captured. He died of his wounds in prison. Ensign James McClure was wounded, and David Flenniker was wounded and carried to a hospital in Charlotte, where he recovered. It would have been a total victory for the Patriots, but the soldiers found rum stored in the outpost and got drunk. They couldn't take prisoners as a result, and most of the British escaped.

On August 16, 1780, General Horatio Gates, the commander of 3,700 American troops, met Lieutenant General Charles Cornwallis with 2,100 British troops about five miles north of Camden, South Carolina, which is located about twenty-five miles northeast of Columbia. Lieutenant Colonel William Polk, son of Colonel Thomas Polk, was the aide-de-camp in the North Carolina State Militia led by Major General Richard Caswell. A Mecklenburg County Regiment of Militia was led by Mecklenburg's Colonel George Alexander and included thirteen companies led by Mecklenburg officers Captain Matthias Beaver; Captain William Gardner; Captain Samuel Givens; Captain Conrad Hise; Captain James Huggins; Captain William Huggins; Captain Nathaniel Marshall Martin; Captain John McFalls; Captain Thomas Shelby, a member of the Rocky River church; Captain Richard Springs; Captain John Sterns; Captain Steel; Captain James White, one of the Mecklenburg Black Boys and a member of the Rocky River church; and Captain David Wilson, a member of the Steele Creek church. William Morrison, a member of the Rocky River church and the son of Neill Morrison, a signer of the Mecklenburg Declaration and a member of the Providence church, was a soldier in one of the units. The American Continental army in the South, most of which had surrendered in Charleston in May 1780, was decimated at Waxham later that same month, when surrendering Patriots were massacred by Lieutenant Colonel Banastre Tarleton. The Patriot army now defending South Carolina was the militia, which was mostly raw recruits with no battle experience. American general Gates made a number of tactical mistakes. He shouldn't have chosen to fight the British in a Loyalist area, where residents wouldn't supply food to his troops and he wouldn't be able to recruit additional men. He didn't provide adequate food and water to his men, and many were too ill to fight because of dysentery. He underestimated the strategic ability of Lieutenant General Cornwallis and put his inexperienced troops on the right flank against the most experienced British troops. It was on the right that his line was broken. And when the left flank also broke, Gates fled with the first of the militia to run from the battle and rode all the way back to Charlotte, sixty miles away. The Americans suffered 900 killed or wounded and 1,000 captured. General Griffith Rutherford was wounded, made a prisoner and held for ten months. William Morrison was wounded by a musket ball and taken prisoner. His mother and sister petitioned for his pardon and got him released. They took him back to Charlotte, where he had the musket ball removed and recovered. In the Battle of Camden, the British had 68 killed, 245 wounded and 11 missing. General Gates never held a field command again but was able to escape a court-martial because of his political connections.

Just two days later, on August 18, General Thomas Sumter and his 700 militiamen and 100 regulars met Lieutenant Colonel Banastre Tarleton and his 100 cavalrymen and 60 light infantrymen at Fishing Creek near present-day Great Falls, South Carolina, about forty miles south of Charlotte. Included in the American troops was a North Carolina Militia detachment with 300 men made up of twelve companies. Four Mecklenburg companies were led by Mecklenburg officers Colonel William Lee Davidson, a member of the Centre church; Captain Francis Miller; Captain Richard Springs; and Captain John Sterns. Following the British victory at Camden, British lieutenant general Cornwallis ordered Tarleton to find Sumter and neutralize his forces. Tarleton left Camden and caught up with Sumter at Fishing Creek, where Sumter was encamped. The British overcame the sentries before they could warn the Patriots. Tarleton's cavalry charged into the surprised camp and captured stands of arms before the Patriots could even get to them. Sumter, who had been sleeping under a wagon, barely escaped. In the Battle of Fishing Creek, more than 150 Americans were killed, while only 16 British were killed or wounded. Tarleton freed British prisoners Sumter had taken the previous two days, as well as capturing 300 Americans.

Because Patriot general Griffith Rutherford was captured at the Battle of Camden, William Lee Davidson was promoted to brigadier general on August 31, 1780, and given Rutherford's former command. The promotion made William Lee Davidson, at age thirty-four, the youngest general to fight in the Revolutionary War.

On September 21, 1780, Colonel William Richardson Davie and 150 Americans surprised Major George Hanger and his 360 British men at

Above: Battle of Camden. *Painting by Alonzo Chappel, National Archives. Courtesy of Wikimedia Commons.*

Left: British colonel Banastre Tarleton. *Painting by Sir Joshua Reynolds, 1782, the National Gallery, London. Courtesy of Wikimedia Commons.*

Wahab's Plantation, about ten miles south of Charlotte. Davie's North Carolina State Cavalry was made up of ten companies, which included seven companies led by Mecklenburg officers Captain Peter Burns; Captain Robert Davis, one of the Mecklenburg Black Boys and a member of the Rocky River church; Captain John Harris, a member of the Steele Creek church; Captain William Hart; Captain Samuel Martin; Captain James Wauchope; and Captain Zaccheus Wilson, a Mecklenburg Declaration signer and an elder of the Steele Creek church. The plantation was owned by Captain James Wauchope, who served as a guide for Davie prior to the attack. Wahab's Plantation was a mispronunciation of Wauchope's name. In the evening, Davie sent a company of men through a cornfield to attack the British in the plantation house, while he and the rest of the troops attacked the camp. In the Battle of Wahab's Plantation, the British were completely surprised, and they suffered 20 men killed and 47 wounded. The rest fled. The Patriots had none killed and 1 man wounded. Davie captured ninety-six horses and 120 muskets and returned to Charlotte.

Five days after returning to Charlotte, Colonel William Richardson Davie learned that the British were advancing on the town on September 26, 1780. Davie and Major James White, one of the Mecklenburg Black Boys and a member of the Rocky River church, commanded the North Carolina State Cavalry–Western District Regiment with seventeen companies, nine of which were led by Mecklenburg officers Captain William Alexander, a member of the Sugaw Creek church; Captain James Byers, a member of the Centre church; Captain William Gardner; Captain Joseph Graham, an elder at the Unity Presbyterian Church, at which Reverend Craighead had been a missionary minister; Captain John Harris, a member of the Steele Creek church; Captain William Hart; Captain David Reed; Captain James Wauchope; and Captain Oliver Wiley, a member of the Rocky River church. Captain Joseph Graham was married to Isabella, the oldest daughter of Captain John Davidson, a Mecklenburg Declaration signer and a member of the Hopewell church. Davie positioned his men around the Mecklenburg County Courthouse. At the time, Charlotte was a small town with about twenty houses and two main streets, which crossed at the courthouse. Davie placed three rows of militia in the front and back of the courthouse, with one behind a stone wall, and positioned cavalry companies on the east and west sides of the courthouse, covering the road leading away from the courthouse in each direction. He also placed twenty men behind a house on the road he believed would be the British approach. An advance guard of British lieutenant general Cornwallis approached the town first.

Even though Cornwallis had ordered Major George Hanger to enter the town with caution, the major had his cavalry gallop into Charlotte. Even after the Patriots behind the house opened fire, Hanger continued to ride forward, at which time his troops were met by heavy fire from the Americans behind the stone wall. Hanger still moved ahead, and his men were caught in crossfire between the second row and the cavalry to the east and west of the courthouse. Hanger was wounded and went down. His cavalry retreated back to Cornwallis's army, which was nearing Charlotte. When Cornwallis's army came into town, Davie made a strategic retreat north toward Salisbury. The British pursued the Americans for about four miles, and near the Sugaw Creek church, Captain Graham turned his men and attacked the British. Graham was severely wounded with nine saber gashes, including four to the head, and he was shot with three musket balls. He almost died, but after crawling a great distance to a house, he had the musket balls removed and recovered from his wounds. Captain Joseph Graham eventually became a major general in the North Carolina Militia, and one of his sons, William A. Graham, became governor of North Carolina in 1845. Lieutenant General Cornwallis later remarked about the "stinging" reception his troops received in Charlotte, saying that the town was the "Hornet's Nest of America." After the war, British colonel Banastre Tarleton wrote that "it was evident, and it has been frequently mentioned to the King's officers, that the counties of Mecklenburg and Rohan [Rowan] were more hostile to England than any other in America." In the Battle of Charlotte, the British had thirty-three men wounded while the Americans had five killed, six wounded and twelve captured. Cornwallis occupied Charlotte for about one week, and during that time, he ordered that the law office and legal books of Waightstill Avery be burned when he learned that Avery was a signer of the Mecklenburg Declaration of Independence. The British were now in control of South Carolina and Georgia and were making plans to conquer North Carolina, but the war would soon turn in the favor of the Americans.

The first sign of the turning of the war toward the Americans was a small skirmish north of Charlotte on October 3, 1780. The troops of Lieutenant General Cornwallis were encamped at Charlotte and running short of food, and a party of at least 460 men was sent out in the countryside to forage for supplies. On that day, Mecklenburg officers Captain James Thompson and Lieutenant George Graham, a brother of Captain Joseph Graham and also a member of the Unity Presbyterian Church, received permission from Brigadier General William Lee Davidson to visit their homes near Charlotte. On discovering the foraging party, the two officers recruited 11 men in the area and attacked the British at McIntyre's Farm on Beattie's Ford Road, north of Charlotte. The 11 Mecklenburg men were Francis Bradley, a member of the Hopewell church; Thomas Dickson; James Henry; George Houston, the son-in-law of Matthew McClure, a Mecklenburg Declaration signer and an elder in the Hopewell church; Hugh Houston; John Long; Thomas McClure, the son of Matthew McClure; John Robinson; Robert Robinson, a member of the Sugaw Creek church; Edward Shipley; and George Shipley. When the Patriots attacked in the Battle of McIntyre's Farm, they killed 8 of the British soldiers, wounded 12 more and forced the foragers to flee back to Charlotte. Musket balls remained obvious on the outside walls of the farmhouse until it was demolished in the 1960s.

British major Patrick Ferguson, with 1,100 Loyalist soldiers, was in the northern part of South Carolina in early October 1780, recruiting for the Loyalist militia and protecting the flank of Cornwallis's army in Charlotte. He had challenged the Patriot militia to give up their arms or suffer the consequences. On hearing the challenge, a number of colonels leading regiments in North Carolina, South Carolina and Virginia decided to attack Ferguson and his militia. Five colonels—William Campbell, John Sevier, Joseph McDowell, Benjamin Cleveland and Isaac Shelby—gathered a force of 1,400 men, which included the Mecklenburg County Regiment of Militia with six companies led by Mecklenburg officers Captain Conrad Hise; Captain James Ligert; Captain Magrath; Captain James Reese;

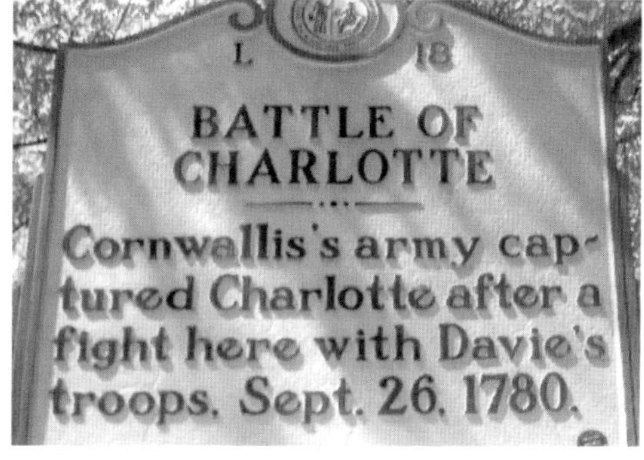

Above: Battle of Charlotte marker. *Photo by author.*

Left: Patriot captain Joseph Graham. *Painting by unknown artist. Courtesy of the North Carolina Portrait Index 1700–1860.*

McIntyre's farm. *Courtesy of the Robinson-Spangler Carolina Room, Charlotte Mecklenburg Library.*

Captain Thomas Shelby, a member of the Rocky River church; and Captain Zaccheus Wilson Sr., a signer of the Mecklenburg Declaration and a member of the Steele Creek church. Mecklenburg officers Lieutenant Colonel Frederick Hambright led the Lincoln County Regiment of Militia; Major James Porter led a North Carolina Militia regiment; and Captain John Brown, a member of the Steele Creek church; Captain John Brandon; Captain William Johnston, a member of the Sugaw Creek church; Captain William Neal, a member of the Centre church; Captain James Porter; Captain Moses Shelby, a member of the Rocky River church; Captain David Vance, a member of the Hopewell church; Captain James White, one of the Mecklenburg Black Boys and a member of the Rocky River church; Lieutenant Andrew Carruthers and Lieutenant James Martin Lewis led companies in the North Carolina Militia. The colonels met and named Colonel William Campbell as their nominal leader but agreed that all 5 would act in council to make decisions. When Major Ferguson heard about the large American force in pursuit of him, he headed back to Charlotte and the protection of Cornwallis's army, but surprisingly, on the night of October 6, he decided to camp on top of King's Mountain, about thirty miles west of Charlotte and only one day's march away. The Patriots put 900 men on horseback, riding through the night and the next morning with constant rain, and the Americans were able to catch up with Ferguson.

The Americans surrounded the mountain and attacked on October 7, 1780. One of the Patriots was John Crockett, father of Davy Crockett. The Patriots charged up the sides of the mountain, firing behind trees and rocks. Initially, the British were taken by surprise. When the Patriots charged, Ferguson had his men charge down the sides of the mountain with fixed bayonets. Since the Americans had no bayonets, they quickly retreated back down the mountain. This pattern kept repeating itself. The top of the mountain at that time was almost treeless, and the Loyalists had no cover, while the Patriots fired from behind rocks and trees. This was an advantage to the Americans. Several of the Patriot regiments reached the top of the mountain and began to attack the Loyalists' rear. After an hour of combat, Loyalist casualties were heavy. Some of his men tried to surrender, but Ferguson cut down their white flags with his sword. Then Ferguson was shot dead with seven bullet holes, and all of the Loyalists began to surrender. It was an important victory for the Patriots. In the Battle of King's Mountain, there were 290 Loyalists killed, 163 wounded and 668 captured. The Americans had 29 killed and 58 wounded. Lieutenant Colonel Frederick Hambright, Captain Moses Shelby and Lieutenant James Martin Lewis were wounded, and Major James Porter died from his wounds. The victory gave a great lift to Patriot morale, it stopped recruitment of Loyalists in the area and it caused Lieutenant General Cornwallis to give up his plans to invade North Carolina. Instead, he left Charlotte and retreated with his troops into South Carolina on October 12.

Colonel Thomas Polk owned a gristmill about two miles southwest of Charlotte that the British were using as a post, from which they sent out foraging parties. On October 9, 1780, Patriot colonel Phillip Taylor led a detachment of about 120 mounted riflemen and found 20 Royal Welsh Fusiliers and a small force of Loyalists stationed at Polk's Mill. Included in Taylor's troops was the North Carolina State Cavalry—Western District Regiment detachment with three companies led by Mecklenburg officers Captain Joseph Graham, recovered from his wounds at the Battle of Charlotte; Captain William Hart; and Captain Zaccheus Wilson Sr., a Mecklenburg Declaration signer and a member of the Steele Creek church. In the Battle of Polk's Mill, the Patriots were able to capture the sentinel of the

Patriots gather for the Battle of King's Mountain. *Painting by Lloyd Branson, 1915, Tennessee State Museum, Nashville. Courtesy of Wikimedia Commons.*

Fusiliers and eight of the Loyalists, but the British drove off the Americans, killing one and wounding another. Later that night, a small group of Patriots returned and stole fifty horses from the British.

In October 1780, General George Washington selected Major General Nathanael Greene as a replacement for General Horatio Gates as commander of the southern army. Greene arrived in Charlotte on December 2 and assumed command on December 3. Greene choose Brigadier General Isaac Huger of South Carolina as his second in command.

On December 4, 1780, Patriot lieutenant colonel William Washington led the Third Regiment of Continental Light Dragoons with about 80 men against a regiment of 114 Loyalists led by Colonel Henry Rugeley at Rugeley's Mills in Cleremont, South Carolina. The colonel was the owner of the mill. Cleremont was located about sixty miles south of Charlotte. Included in Washington's regiment were three companies of the Mecklenburg County Regiment detachment led by Mecklenburg officers Captain James Byers, a member of the Centre church; Captain Francis Miller; and Captain John Sterns. Washington had no artillery, so he ordered musket fire on the fortified barn, which was surrounded by a ditch and felled trees with sharpened branches. The musket fire did very little damage. Washington then had his men make a fake cannon out of a pine log and put it in view of the Loyalists. He then demanded that the Loyalists surrender or be fired upon with the cannon. In the Battle of Rugeley's Mills, Colonel Rugeley surrendered to the Americans, and the 114 Loyalists were made prisoners but later paroled.

The Patriots burned down the barn and returned to Hanging Rock and then to Camp New Providence, south of Charlotte, where they learned that Major General Nathanael Greene was their new commander.

Patriot brigadier general Daniel Morgan reported for duty at Major General Nathanael Greene's headquarters in Charlotte on December 3, 1780. Greene decided to split his army, which was unusual, and sent Morgan and his 600 men to the west on December 21 to join the militia west of the Catawba River. Greene believed this would raise the morale of the militia and help find additional recruits. Morgan then went into South Carolina and was joined there by militia from that state and Georgia, bringing his total force to 1,912 men, which included the Mecklenburg County Regiment of Militia detachment led by Mecklenburg officers Captain John Irby and Captain James Nathaniel Martin, a member of the Rocky River church. Two other Mecklenburg officers were in other counties' regiments, Captain William Alexander, a member of the Sugaw Creek church, and Captain Moses Shelby, a member of the Rocky River church. In early January, British lieutenant general Charles Cornwallis ordered Lieutenant Colonel

Polk's Mill millstones, Revolution Park. *Photo by author.*

Banastre Tarleton with his 1,150 men to find Morgan's army and attack it. Tarleton caught up with Morgan on January 17, 1781, at Cowpens, South Carolina, about fifty-five miles southwest of Charlotte. Morgan went against usual battle strategy and placed his men between the Broad and Pacolet Rivers, which meant escape in the event of retreat was impossible. He did this to ensure that his untrained militiamen would not run but stay and fight with his Continental soldiers if the battle became rough. He placed his Continentals on a small hill in the center, where he believed Tarleton would attack. Morgan also set up three lines with his sharpshooters in the first line, militiamen in the second and the Continentals in the third. He ordered the militia to fire only three volleys when the attack came and then withdraw to the left and reform behind the third line. Tarleton's men were exhausted, with less than four hours of sleep and no food in two days, and Tarleton was overconfident of victory. Morgan's plan worked to perfection. Tarleton attacked in the center, and the third Continental line was hidden by the first two lines. When both of the first two lines withdrew, the British charged forward, thinking the Patriots were in a full retreat, and found themselves fighting the unexpected Continentals uphill. The Continentals fired into the British no more than thirty yards away and then mounted a bayonet charge at them. British casualties were great, and they began to surrender in large numbers. The Americans then seized the British cannons, which Tarleton attempted to save with about 40 cavalrymen, but they had to retreat. As he did, the Patriots' Colonel Washington was close enough to ask, "Where is now the boasting Tarleton?" Tarleton shot the horse from under Washington and fled, and the battle ended. In the Battle of Cowpens, the Americans killed 110 British and took 712 prisoners, which included 200 wounded. The Americans had 25 killed and 124 wounded. Cowpens was an important victory for the Patriots.

When Morgan was sent west and then into South Carolina, Major General Nathanael Greene led his 1,100 malnourished and sick men to rest on the Pee Dee River near Cheraw, South Carolina, about 65 miles southeast of Charlotte. Greene knew that his men were in no condition to fight unless given rest and nourishment, and the area was abundant in fish and game. Greene called the location his Camp of Repose. He stayed there for a month and then headed back to Charlotte. Greene met up with Morgan and his army heading back north after the Cowpens victory on the Beattie's Ford Road, about twenty miles north of Charlotte, on January 30, 1781. Greene knew that Lieutenant General Cornwallis and his army of 5,000 men were in close pursuit, chasing Morgan. He and his officers agreed they were not ready to stand and fight against such superior numbers and decided to make a strategic retreat into Virginia and across the Dan River, about 145 miles to the north. The retreat was called the Race to the Dan and was an important strategy in the eventual victory of the American forces. The strategy worked because Greene had the foresight to have boats built when he had first arrived in Charlotte, knowing that North Carolina had many rivers that would need to be crossed. Greene also ordered that Colonel Otho Williams and his 700 light troops play a decoy by heading toward the shallow fords on the Catawba River, making Cornwallis think that's how the main Patriot army would cross rivers. Cornwallis took the bait and pursued Williams, while Greene's main army crossed the Catawba down the river in boats.

Greene also ordered Brigadier General William Lee Davidson to slow Cornwallis's advance by placing his men at various fords along the Catawba River on the far banks. Davidson's men included the Mecklenburg County Regiment of Militia with ten companies led by Mecklenburg officers Lieutenant Colonel William Polk, the son of Colonel Thomas Polk. Nine of those companies were led by Mecklenburg officers Captain William Alexander, a member of the Sugaw Creek church; Captain Joseph Graham,

Battle of Cowpens. *Engraved for* Garham's Magazine *by S.H. Gimber, 1931, National Archives and Records Administration. Courtesy of Wikimedia Commons.*

an elder in the Unity Presbyterian Church; Captain Conrad Hise; Captain James Huggins; Captain James Ligert; Captain Samuel Martin; Captain James Maxwell; and Captain Charles Polk, brother of Colonel Thomas Polk. The Rowan County Regiment of Militia detachment with thirteen companies was led by Mecklenburg officer Major James Hall, and the Lincoln County Regiment of Militia detachment with six companies was led by Mecklenburg officer Major David Wilson, a member of the Steele Creek church. Davidson placed most of his men at Beattie's Ford and placed a company of cavalry and infantry four miles south at Cowan's Ford to make sure the British did not make a surprise crossing there at night. In the evening of February 1, 1781, Davidson joined his men at Cowan's Ford. Near daybreak, the British began crossing Cowan's Ford, choosing to go across at the shorter but deeper ford rather than the longer but shallower horse ford. Soon the swollen river was over the heads of the British horses, and the Patriots began shooting the British cavalrymen in the water. The British on the banks returned heavy fire, and Davidson was shot through the heart by a rifle ball and fell off his horse. When Davidson was killed, the Americans, now led by Lieutenant Colonel William Polk, retreated, while Captain Joseph Graham and his men protected their retreat. The Patriots were successful in that they slowed the advance of Cornwallis's army in the race to the Dan River. In the Battle of Cowan's Ford, four Americans were

Above: Camp New Providence marker. *Photo by author.*

Left: Patriot major general Nathanael Greene. *Painting by Charles Willson Peale, 1784, Independence National Park, Philadelphia. Courtesy of Wikimedia Commons.*

killed, including Davidson and Major James Hall, and three captured, while the British had four killed and thirty-six wounded. Major David Wilson and two other men later recovered Davidson's body, which had been stripped naked by the British. Davidson's body was taken to his house, and his wife decided it was best to bury him at the Hopewell church rather than at his own Centre church because they were afraid the British might further desecrate the body.

On February 2, 1781, Lieutenant General Cornwallis ordered Lieutenant Colonel Banastre Tarleton to find the Patriots retreating from Cowan's Ford. He captured several retreating Americans and learned that the Patriots would be gathering at Tarrant's Tavern at 2:00 p.m. that day. About twenty-seven companies of Americans met at Tarrant's Tavern and began drinking heavily, including the Mecklenburg County Regiment of Militia, with two companies led by Mecklenburg officers Captain Joseph Graham and Captain James Huggins. Even though Lieutenant Tarleton was greatly outnumbered, he charged the Patriots, most of whom fled with their buckets of rum. Captain Salathiel Martin, who led a company in another county's regiment, attempted to organize the men and make a stand behind a fence but wasn't very successful. The British shot Captain Martin's horse, and he was captured. In the Battle of Tarrant's Tavern, ten Americans were killed and an unknown number wounded. It is also unknown how many of the British were killed or wounded. Cornwallis ordered the tavern burned down the next day.

As Cornwallis pursued Greene and his army of 1,600 men in the Race to the Dan, he was continuously slowed because Greene was able to cross rivers in his boats, while Cornwallis had to move along the rivers until he found shallow fords for his men to cross. Greene also ordered Colonel Carrington, who was posted in Richmond, Virginia, to go south to the Dan River and find one hundred boats and hide them along the banks of the Dan near Boyd's and Irwin's Ferries. Colonel Williams was doing a good job of harassing and slowing Cornwallis's army, but in spite of this, Cornwallis was still closing in on Greene. Because of the close pursuit, when Greene reached the Dan River, he hired four ferrymen to ferry men, horses and wagons across the river to supplement the one hundred boats hidden along the banks. Greene had arrived at the Dan on the afternoon of February 13, and by the afternoon of February 14, all the men, horses and wagons were across the river. When Colonel Williams received word that most of Green's army was across, he and his men turned and raced for the Dan themselves. Six hours after Colonel Williams crossed the river, Cornwallis arrived at the

Dan, but all the boats and ferries were on the other side. In frustration, Cornwallis ordered his cannons fired across the river, but Green's army had moved on to Halifax, Virginia. There was no way Cornwallis could pursue the Americans. Over the next month, Greene was able to build his army to about 2,600 men with new recruits, and he then decided he was ready to take on Cornwallis's army.

Major General Greene sent Brigadier General Andrew Pickens and his men on a mission to Hillsborough, North Carolina, about forty-five miles south of Halifax to gather intelligence, inhibit Loyalist recruitment and engage the British when it was feasible. Pickens's forces included the Mecklenburg County Regiment of Militia, with twenty-five cavalrymen and twenty infantrymen led by Captain Joseph Graham. Pickens sent Captain Graham and his men out to determine the British positions around Hillsborough. About one and a half miles from Hillsborough, Captain Graham discovered a British detachment at Hart's Mill on the Eno River, not far from where Cornwallis's army was camped. At dawn on February 17, 1781, Graham attacked the mill, completely surprising the British. He captured sixteen British regulars and two Loyalists. In the Battle of Hart's Mill, nine British were killed or wounded. No Americans were killed, and an unknown number were wounded. The prisoners were marched back to Halifax, Virginia.

Greene then sent Lieutenant Colonel Henry "Lighthorse Harry" Lee, father of Robert E. Lee, with about 1,300 men toward Burlington, North Carolina, with the same mission as Pickens. Included in Lee's men were Mecklenburg officers Captain James Byers, a member of the Centre church, and Captain Joseph Graham in charge of two companies of men in the Lincoln County Regiment of Militia detachment and a Mecklenburg County Regiment of Militia detachment with two companies led by Mecklenburg officers Captain William Alexander, a member of the Sugaw Creek church, and

William Lee Davidson marker. *Photo by author.*

Captain James Reese. On February 25, 1781, near the town of Haw River, Lee and his dragoon mounted men came across two young advance scouts of reinforcements that British lieutenant general Cornwallis was sending to Lieutenant Colonel Banastre Tarleton, who was camped about two miles away. The scouts were looking for Tarleton's camp and thought that Lee's dragoons were Tarleton's men because both dressed in green coats. Lee told the scouts to go back and join their reinforcement troops with "Colonel Tarleton's compliments," and requested that the reinforcements move off the road to allow "Tarleton's cavalry to pass." Lee had Captain Eggleston's cavalry circle through the woods and Captain Graham's company follow a short distance after his men because they weren't dressed in green coats. When they came upon the British reinforcements of about 400 men led by Colonel John Pyle, the British were on the right side of the road in review formation. Lee nodded and smiled at the British soldiers, and he stopped in front of Pyle, who saluted Lee. Lee saluted back, and they shook hands. Some of the British soldiers noticed Eggleston's men in the woods and, without a command, opened fire on them. Eggleston's cavalry charged at the British, firing their muskets and slashing at them with their swords. Colonel Pyle, still confused, yelled out, "Stop! Stop! You are killing your own men!" Then a Patriot sword knocked Pyle off his horse, and the British surrendered. In the Battle of Haw River, the British had 99 killed, 150 wounded and about 100 captured. The Americans had only 1 man wounded. One of the captured men was brought in front of Lieutenant Colonel Lee, and the man still believed that Lee was Tarleton. The man declared, "God bless your soul! Mr. Tarleton, you've just killed as good a parcel of subjects as His Majesty ever had!" Lee exclaimed in response, "You damned rascal! We are Americans, not British. I am Lee of the American Legion!" Some of the British reached Tarleton's camp and told him what had happened. Tarleton realized he couldn't take on the Patriots without reinforcements, so he fled back to Cornwallis's camp at Hillsborough.

On March 2, 1781, troops under Lieutenant Colonel Banastre Tarleton were foraging near Clapp's Mill on Alamance Creek about four miles southwest of Burlington, North Carolina. They were discovered by about eight hundred American men led by Brigadier General Andrew Pickens, which included a company headed by Mecklenburg's Captain Joseph Graham with twenty-five men. Pickens positioned his men in thickets on each side of the road that he believed would be used by the British. As they approached, the Americans opened fire, causing heavy casualties. The Patriots were finally driven back, but in the Battle of Clapp's Mill, Tarleton's forces had twenty-five men killed or wounded, while Pickens's forces had ten or twelve men killed or wounded, including Mecklenburg soldiers John Ford and David Johnston, who were killed. The day after the Clapp's Mill engagement, Pickens sent out Captain Joseph Graham with twenty-five cavalry to see if the British were still on the battlefield, and Graham found that they had left after burying their dead. Graham rode up within a half mile of the British line and sent a sergeant and six men back to Pickens to relate the British position. During the night, Graham moved his men through the woods to capture two sentries he had seen in the evening. The sentries heard his approach and fired on the Americans. A squad of British soldiers was sent to look into the shooting. They thought Graham's men were British and hailed them, were fired on at point-blank range and driven back. Captain Graham captured the officer of the squad.

Colonel Otho H. Williams and his seven hundred men, including the Mecklenburg County Regiment of Militia detachment with a company led by Captain Joseph Graham, came within a mile of the British camp of Lieutenant Colonel Banastre Tarleton on March 2. Tarleton had a force of one thousand men, who were camped south of Burlington, North Carolina, on the Haw River. When he learned that the Americans were near, Tarleton decided to make an attack on Lieutenant Colonel Henry Lee's legion of six companies, which was separated from Pickens's main force. It was a brief but difficult skirmish for the British. They had casualties of thirty men killed or wounded, while the Americans had no losses. Then Tarleton met Colonel Williams's full force at Whitesell's Mill, which was located twelve miles northeast of Greensboro on March 6, 1781, at 8:00 a.m. The mill was owned by Patriot captain Henry Whitesell of the Guilford County Regiment of militia, which was also in the battle. The British attacked the Americans, and the Patriots returned the fire but then fled across Alamance Creek. The British infantry followed them across the creek and were met with a severe attack in return. The British infantry was supported by four artillery pieces placed on a hill near the creek, which convinced the Americans to retreat. Tarleton decided not to pursue the Patriots. In the Battle of Whitesell's Mill, the British had thirty men killed or wounded, while the Patriots had eight killed and twelve wounded.

Lieutenant General Charles Cornwallis was camped with his 1,900 British men on Deep River, twelve miles west of Greensboro, North Carolina, and he learned that 4,400 Americans under Major General Nathanael Greene were at Guilford Court House, seven miles northwest of the city. Despite his smaller army, Cornwallis decided to attack the Patriots. Included in the

Battle of Clapp's Mill marker. *Photo by author.*

American men were Colonel William Richardson Davie, who was on Greene's senior staff; two Mecklenburg County Militia companies led by Mecklenburg officers Captain John Brown, a member of the Steele Creek church, and Captain Robert Smith; a Mecklenburg County detachment with eight companies led by Captain Stephen Alexander, a member of the Popular Tent church, Captain Conrad Hise, Captain James Ligert, Captain Francis Miller, Captain Jonathan Potts, Captain Thomas Ray, Captain John Rogers and Captain David Wilson, a member of the Steele Creek church; a Rowan County regiment with five detachments and eight companies with second in command Major Ezekiel Polk, brother of Mecklenburg Declaration signer Colonel Thomas Polk; and a company of Mecklenburg County Mounted Minutemen led by Captain John Reid. On March 15, 1781, there was a brief engagement of Lieutenant Colonel Henry Lee's American Dragoons with Lieutenant Colonel Banastre Tarleton's British Dragoons about four miles away from the Guilford Court House. The Cornwallis army found Green's men about one and a half miles from the courthouse on rising ground in three defensive lines. The North Carolina Militia was on the first line behind a picket fence with a six-pound cannon on each side of the road, the Virginia militia on the second line and the regulars on the third line with two more six-pound cannons in the center. The lines were hundreds of yards apart. At 1:30 p.m., Cornwallis advanced to within 150 yards of the first line, which made a short barrage of cannon fire and a volley of long gunfire. The British advanced farther so that their shorter-range muskets were close enough to fire a volley in return. The British then advanced to within fifty paces of the first line, which could use deadly aim with their long guns resting on the picket fence. The British still continued to advance, and the first line fled back into the woods. The British advanced all the way to the third line with great losses, captured the four six-pound cannons and forced the Americans to retreat. The Battle of Guilford Court House lasted only ninety minutes but was deadly. The

Battle of Guilford Court House. *Painting by H. Charles McBarron Jr., United States Army Center of Military History. Courtesy of Wikimedia Commons.*

British had the victory, but they lost over a quarter of their men. They had 5 officers and 88 men killed, 24 officers and 389 men wounded and 26 men missing. Cornwallis had his horse shot from under him. The Americans had 79 killed, 184 wounded and 1,046 missing. Greene decided to retreat to Charlotte and then on to South Carolina. Cornwallis decided not to pursue the Patriots and headed back to Hillsborough. A few weeks later, Cornwallis marched his men to Wilmington on the coast to recruit more Loyalists and resupply his army.

Major General Nathanael Greene decided in April 1781 to move on the remaining British outposts in South Carolina and force them back to Charleston. He first marched on Camden, South Carolina, about seventy miles south of Charlotte, since it was at the center of the outposts. He had 1,551 men under his command, including the Mecklenburg County Regiment of Militia detachment with one company led by Mecklenburg's Captain William Nesbitt. When Greene was one and a half miles north of Camden, he decided to camp on a ridge called Hobkirk's Hill. He knew he didn't have enough men to attack Camden, and he hoped he could draw out the British to attack his position. Greene organized the camp so that battle positions could be quickly formed if they were attacked. Colonel Francis Rawdon and his 900 British soldiers took the bait and attacked the hill on April 25, 1781. The American artillery produced heavy casualties, but the British were able to force the Americans off the ridge, and the Patriots retreated for a few miles. In the Battle of Hobkirk's Hill, the British had 38 killed and 258 wounded. The Patriots had 18 killed and 248 wounded or missing. A tactical victory was won by the British, but the Americans won a strategic victory because Rawdon marched most of his men back to Charleston, leaving only a company of dragoons at Hobkirk's Hill. The next day, Greene returned to the battlefield, drove off the British dragoons and rescued the wounded Americans and the stragglers.

By mid-May 1781, the only locations in South Carolina with significant British influence were Charleston and Ninety Six, which was located about forty-five miles southeast of Greenville. The British outpost at Ninety Six was defended by 550 Loyalists under the command of Lieutenant Colonel John Cruger. The fort was surrounded by a deep ditch, felled trees with sharpened branches and three three-pound cannons. Major General Nathanael Greene led more than 1,000 men, including the First North Carolina Regiment of Continentals detachment with 66 men in four companies, one of which was led by Captain Alexander Brevard, brother of Dr. Ephraim Brevard, a Mecklenburg Declaration signer and an elder of the Hopewell church, and a company in the First South Carolina Regiment of State Dragoons detachment led by Captain William Alexander, a member of the Sugaw Creek church. Greene realized that the fort was too well fortified to attack, so he started a twenty-eight-day siege that began on May 22, 1781. Greene's men dug a trench within thirty yards of the fort and built a thirty-foot tower with a protected platform on the top. From the tower, sharpshooting riflemen were able to pick off British artillerymen. Colonel Cruger had his British men add sandbags to raise the height of the parapet, and his men were able to fire through openings in the sandbags at the tower. He also tried to set the tower on fire with heated shot but couldn't make the balls hot enough. The Americans attempted to set the fort on fire with flaming arrows, but that proved unsuccessful. On June 6, Greene learned that Colonel Francis Rawdon had left Charleston with 2,000 men and was coming to Ninety Six to aid Cruger, and Greene decided to attack the fort on June 19. His plan was to get enough men inside the fort to pull down the sandbags, so the tower could fire on the men inside. It worked, but Cruger launched a counterattack, and the battle became one of bayonets and muskets used as clubs. The Americans were forced to retreat, and with Colonel Francis Rawdon only thirty miles away, Greene decided to retreat back to Charlotte. In the Siege of Ninety-Six, the Americans had 57 killed, 70 wounded and 20 missing, while the British had 27 killed and 58 wounded. Even though the fort was saved, Colonel Rawdon made the decision to burn it and take the remaining men back to Charleston. The Americans had accomplished their goal. Rawdon was in poor health and went back to England in August 1781, leaving Charleston in the command of Colonel Alexander Stewart.

Major General Greene decided in August to march toward Charleston with 2,000 men, including the First North Carolina Regiment with two companies led by Mecklenburg officers Captain Alexander Brevard and Captain Griffith John McRee, a member of the Steele Creek church; the Mecklenburg County Regiment of Militia detachment with a company led by Mecklenburg officer Captain John Sterns; the South Carolina First Regiment of State Dragoons with six companies, three led by Mecklenburg officers Captain William Alexander, a member of the Sugaw Creek church, Captain Samuel Martin and Captain Thomas Polk, son of Colonel Thomas Polk. Colonel Alexander Stewart, the commander of 2,000 British soldiers in Charleston, learned of Greene's march and decided to find the Americans. He made an encampment at Eutaw Springs, which was about fifty miles northwest of Charleston. Greene had been camping for over two weeks only seven miles away, north of the Santee River, because he wanted his men to be well rested for battle. Finding out that Stewart was camped at Eutaw Springs, Greene had his army of 1,900 infantry, 300 cavalry, two three-pound cannons and two six-pound cannons leave his camp at 4:00 a.m. on September 8, 1781, and march toward Stewart's camp.

At about 8:00 a.m., a mounted American scouting party encountered a British cavalry reconnoitering unit. The British pursued the Americans but were led into an ambush. The British cavalry officer escaped, but 4 or 5 British were killed and 40 captured. The American mounted unit then found an unarmed group of British foragers and captured 400 of them. The British cavalry officer went back to Stewart and told him of the Americans approaching. Stewart led his army toward the Patriots. Greene formed his men into two lines, with the militia in the front and the regulars behind. The British charged and broke through the center of the first line and then advanced through the center of the second line. The American flanks came in support and were able to drive the British in a disordered retreat back to their camp. The British were able to reorganize at a brick house at their camp and counterattacked the Patriots, who retreated in an orderly manner. Since the Americans eventually had to retreat, it was considered a tactical victory for the British, but it was a strategic victory for the Americans. In the Battle of Eutaw Springs, the British had 85 killed, 297 wounded, 70 wounded prisoners and 430 captured. The Americans had 119 killed, 382 wounded, 60 captured and 18 missing. Captain Thomas Polk, son of Colonel Thomas Polk, was among the Americans killed. Stewart withdrew his troops back to Charleston a day after the battle. Eutaw Springs was the last major battle in the Carolinas.

On October 1, 1781, Brigadier General Griffith Rutherford and his Patriot army, which included the North Carolina State Legion detachment with second in command Major Joseph Graham, an elder of the Unity Presbyterian Church, and four companies marched toward Wilmington, North Carolina. His army encircled Wilmington and slowly constricted it. During the siege of Wilmington, Lieutenant Colonel Henry Lee's Legion brought word of the surrender of the British at Yorktown, Virginia, on October 19. General George Washington had captured seven thousand British men, including Lieutenant General Charles Cornwallis. The British commander at Wilmington, Major James Craig, was given orders to evacuate the town by sea and take the troops to Charleston, which he did on November 18, 1781. As the last of the British troops were marching to the boats, Rutherford led his men into Wilmington. One of the Loyalists held out his hand, intending to salute the Americans, but a cavalryman named Thomas Tyler drew out his sword and split the Loyalist's head open. It was later learned that what seemed like a barbaric act had a cause. The Loyalist had hanged Tyler's father. That was the only death in the siege and evacuation of Wilmington.

Emboldened by the surrender at Yorktown, Major General Greene soon surrounded Charleston with a number of encampments within a thirty-mile radius of the city. It was obvious the British were no longer attempting to wage war in America, so there was no need to attack the city. It took over a year for the British to leave, but finally, on December 14, 1782, they evacuated Charleston by ship and sailed to England. The negotiations between the United States and Great Britain were finally concluded on September 3, 1783, in the Treaty of Paris, in which Great Britain recognized the United States to be free, sovereign and independent states. Reverend Alexander Craighead had achieved his goal seventeen years after his death.

Cornwallis Surrenders at Yorktown. *Painting by John Trumbull, 1820, Rotunda of U.S. Capitol, Washington, D.C. Courtesy of Wikimedia Commons.*

Appendix

LIST OF MECKLENBURG COUNTY REVOLUTIONARY WAR SOLDIERS

ADAMS, WILLIAM

ALEXANDER, COLONEL ABRAHAM
Mecklenburg Declaration signer
elder, Sugaw Creek church

ALEXANDER, COLONEL ADAM
Mecklenburg Declaration signer
Elder, Rocky River church

ALEXANDER, CAPTAIN CHARLES, FOURTH NORTH CAROLINA

ALEXANDER, CHARLES, JR.

ALEXANDER, DAN

ALEXANDER, EZEKIEL

ALEXANDER, CAPTAIN EZRA
Mecklenburg Declaration signer

ALEXANDER, COLONEL GEORGE

ALEXANDER, FIRST LIEUTENANT HEZEKIAH, FOURTH NORTH CAROLINA
Mecklenburg Declaration signer
elder, Hopewell church

ALEXANDER, ISAAC
Sugaw Creek church

ALEXANDER, CAPTAIN JAMES
Steele Creek church

ALEXANDER, ENSIGN JOHN
Hopewell church

ALEXANDER, CAPTAIN JOHN MCNITT
Mecklenburg Declaration signer
elder, Hopewell church

ALEXANDER, COLONEL NATHANIEL
Sugaw Creek church

ALEXANDER, CAPTAIN STEPHEN
Poplar Tent church

ALEXANDER, MAJOR THOMAS
Sugaw Creek church

ALEXANDER, CAPTAIN THOMAS
Sugaw Creek church

ALEXANDER, WILLIAM, SR.
Sugaw Creek church

ALEXANDER, WILLIAM
Sugaw Creek church

ALEXANDER, WILLIAM BAIN
Hopewell church

ALEXANDER, CAPTAIN WILLIAM LEE, NORTH CAROLINA REGIMENT
Rocky River church
ALEXANDER, LIEUTENANT WILLIAM S., FOURTH NORTH CAROLINA
Rocky River church
ALLEN, JOHN
ALLEN, CAPTAIN THOMAS, First North Carolina
ALLEN, FIRST LIEUTENANT THOMAS, THIRD NORTH CAROLINA
taken prisoner at Charleston May 12, 1780
died in prison August 26, 1780
ALLISON, COLONEL JOHN, NORTH CAROLINA MILITIA
wounded at Stono Ferry June 20, 1779
Polar Tent church
ALSTON, COLONEL WILLIAM
ANDREW, WILLIAM
Rocky River church
ASHE, CAPTAIN SAMUEL, JR., FIRST NORTH CAROLINA DRAGOONS

BAIRD, COLONEL ANDREW
BARNET, JOHN, SR.
BARNET, JOHN
BARRINGER, CAPTAIN JOHN
BARRY, ANDREW
BARRY, CAPTAIN RICHARD
Mecklenburg Declaration signer
elder, Hopewell church
BEAVER, CAPTAIN MATTHIAS
BENJAMIN, JONATHAN
BERRYHILL, LIEUTENANT WILLIAM, FIRST NORTH CAROLINA
Steele Creek church
BEST, JOHN
BIGGER, ROBERT
Rocky River church
BIGHAM, JOSEPH
BINGHAM, SEPTEMIAS
BLACK, EZEAKEL
BLACK, JOHN
Rocky River church
BLACK, ENSIGN JOHN
BLACK, CAPTAIN THOMAS
BLACKWELDER, ISAAC
BOSWELL, RUBIN
BOYD, PATRICK
BRADLEY, FRANCIS
BRADSHAW, JAMES
Rocky River church
BRADSHAW, JOHN
Rocky River church
BRANDON, CAPTAIN JOHN, NORTH CAROLINA MILITIA
BREVARD, COLONEL ALEXANDER, NORTH CAROLINA MILITIA
brother of Dr. Ephraim Brevard
BREVARD, SURGEON EPHRAIM, FIRST NORTH CAROLINA
Mecklenburg Declaration signer
elder, Hopewell church
taken prisoner at Charleston May 12, 1780
exchanged June 14, 1781
died 1781
BREVARD, FIRST LIEUTENANT JOHN, NINTH NORTH CAROLINA
Centre church
BRITTON, JAMES

Brown, Benjamin
Rocky River

Brown, Lieutenant Colonel James S., North Carolina Militia
taken prisoner in 1778

Brown, James
Rocky River church

Brown, James
Rocky River church

Brown, James
Steele Creek church

Brown, Captain John, First North Carolina
Steele Creek church

Brown, William

Brown, William

Brownfield, Captain John

Buckaloe, Jonathan

Bucklaw, Garrot

Bucklaw, George

Bucklaw, James

Bucklaw, Jonathan

Burns, James
Rocky River church

Burns, Captain Porter

Byers, Captain James
Centre church

Calberson, Captain Jonathan

Caldwell, Captain David
Rocky River church

Caldwell, James

Caldwell, John
Rocky River church

Caldwell, Captain Samuel
Sugaw Creek church

Campbell, Andrew
Rocky River church

Campbell, Charles
Rocky River church

Campbell, Captain James, Fifth North Carolina
wounded and captured at Stono Ferry June 20, 1779
exchanged June 14, 1781

Campbell, John
Sugaw Creek church

Campbell, William
Rocky River church

Carithers, John

Carothers, John
Rocky River church

Carothers, Robert
Mecklenburg Black Boys
Rocky River church

Carpenter, Lieutenant Christian

Carruthers, Lieutenant Andrew, North Carolina Militia

Carter, Henry

Caruthers, Colonel John

Casiah, Dunning

Ciswell, Lieutenant Andrew

Clark, Cornolus

Clark, James

Cochran, Benjamin
Mecklenburg Black Boys
Rocky River church

Cochran, John
Rocky River church

Cochran, Robert
Rocky River church

Cochran, William
Rocky River church

COLLINS, MAJOR BRUCE
COLLINS, CAPTAIN JACOB
taken prisoner at Charleston May 12, 1780
exchanged June 14, 1781
CONNOR, JAMES
COX, JOHN
CRAIGHEAD, CAPTAIN ROBERT, NORTH CAROLINA MILITIA
son of Reverend Alexander Craighead
Sugaw Creek church
wounded at Hanging Rock August 6, 1780
CRAWFORD, GEORGE
CROMISLE, CAPTAIN
CUMMINS, JOHN
CUNNINGHAM, WILLIAM

DAVIDSON, MAJOR JOHN
Mecklenburg Declaration signer
Hopewell church
DAVIDSON, LIEUTENANT THOMAS, NORTH CAROLINA MILITIA
DAVIDSON, BRIGADIER GENERAL WILLIAM LEE, NORTH CAROLINA MILITIA
Centre church
wounded at Colson's Mill July 21, 1780
killed at Cowan's Ford
DAVIE, COLONEL WILLIAM RICHARDSON, NORTH CAROLINA CAVALRY
wounded at Stono Ferry June 20, 1779
DAVIES, GEORGE
Sugaw Creek church
DAVIES, ROBERT
DAVIES, THOMAS
DAVIS, JAMES
DAVIS, JOHN
Rocky River church
DAVIS, JOHN L.
DAVIS, CAPTAIN ROBERT
Mecklenburg Black Boys
Rocky River church
DAVIS, THOMAS
Rock River church
DAVIS, LIEUTENANT COLONEL WILLIAM, FIRST NORTH CAROLINA
DAVIS, WILLIAM
DICKSON, JOHN
Rocky River church
DICKSON, THOMAS
DORTON, CHARLES
Rocky River church
DORTON, WILLIAM
DOWNS, THOMAS
DRISKILL, WILLIAM
DUCK, JOHN
Rocky River church
DUSENBURY, SAMUEL

Edminson, James
Elm, Charles, Sr.
Erwin, Captain Alexander

Ferguson, Alexander
Rocky River church
Ferguson, Thomas
Rocky River church
Ferrill, Gabriel
Findley, Charles
Findley, John
Flanagan, Captain Samuel
Flenken, David, Sr.
Flenniker, David
wounded at Hanging Rock August 6, 1780, and carried to Charlotte hospital
Flennikin, David
Flough, David
Foard, Sergeant John, North Carolina Dragoons
Rocky River church
Ford, John
Forney, Captain Jacob
Forney, Captain Peter, North Carolina Rangers
Foster, Captain John
Frederick, Philip

Gailbraith, Robert
Gailbraith, William
Gardner, Captain James, Second North Carolina
Gardner, Second Lieutenant William, Second North Carolina
Garrat, Thomas
Garrison, David
Gaseway, Captain John, Sixth North Carolina
Gentry, Captain Meshack
Givens, Captain Samuel
Glover, John
Goodwin, Robert
Gourley, Thomas
Rocky River church
Graham, Captain George, North Carolina Rangers
Unity church
Graham, Major Joseph, North Carolina Rangers
elder, Unity church
wounded at Charlotte September 26, 1780
Graham, Captain Richard, Second North Carolina
Graham, Colonel William
Hopewell church
Graham, William
Grible, Thomas

Hadley, Captain Joshua, First North Carolina
Hagan, Lieutenant Colonel John William
Hall, Lieutenant James, North Carolina Militia
killed at Cowan's Ford February 1, 1781
Hall, John
Hall, Second Lieutenant Thomas, First North Carolina
Hambright, Lieutenant Colonel Frederick, North Carolina Militia
wounded at King's Mountain October 7, 1780
Hardision, Captain Benjamin
Harris, George
Harris, Colonel James
Philadelphia church
Harris, Jeremiah
Harris, Captain John
Steele Creek church
Harris, Joseph
Harris, Colonel Robert, Sr.
elder, Popular Tent church
Harris, Captain Robert
Rocky River church
Harris, Major Samuel, Sr.
Rocky River church
Harris, Samuel, Jr.
Rocky River church
Harris, Major Thomas, Fourth North Carolina
Rocky River church
Harris, William
Rocky River church
Hart, Captain William
Hayone, William
Hays, First Lieutenant Robert, First North Carolina
taken prisoner at Charleston May 12, 1780
exchanged June 14, 1781
Headley, Joshua
Mecklenburg Black Boys
Rocky River church
Henry, Lieutenant James
Hill, Lieutenant John, Tenth North Carolina
Steele Creek church
Hill, Robert
Hise, Captain Conrad
Holton, Thomas
Houghup, James
Houston, George
Houston, Hugh
Houston, Captain Isaac
Houston, Captain James, Rangers
wounded at Ramsour's Mill June 20, 1780
Centre church
Hovie, Samuel
Rocky River church
Howard, William
Howard, William
Howell, Burdick
Howell, James
Huddleston, Robert
Huggins, Captain James
Huggins, Captain William
Hughes, Samuel
Hunter, Humphrey
Steele Creek church
Hutchinson, Captain William

Irby, Captain John
Irwin, Captain Robert
Mecklenburg Declaration signer
Steele Creek church
Irwin, Thomas
Rocky River church
Irwin, William

Jack, Captain James
Mecklenburg Declaration carrier
elder, Providence church
Johnston, David
Johnston, Captain John, North Carolina Militia
Johnston, Nathaniel
Rocky River church
Johnston, Captain William, North Carolina Militia
Sugaw Creek church
Johnston, William
Jones, Isaac N.
Sugaw Creek church

Kennon, Lieutenant William, First North Carolina
Mecklenburg Declaration signer
Kerr, Joseph
Hopewell church
Kerr, Robert
Kilpatrick, Hugh
Rocky River church
Kimmons, Alexander
Rocky River church
Kincaid, Robert
Knox, Captain James
Hopewell church
Knox, Captain Patrick
killed at Ramsour's Mill June 20, 1780

Lacey, Ensign Samuel
Lackey, Thomas
Lawson, Lieutenant John, Ninth North Carolina
Lemmon, Second Lieutenant John
Lemmon, Surgeon William
Lewis, Lieutenant James Martin, North Carolina Militia
wounded at King's Mountain October 7, 1780
Ligert, Captain James
Liggit, Lieutenant William
Linsay, Drummer Hugh
Steele Creek church
Linton, Samuel
Locke, Captain John
Long, Captain John
Long, John
Love, Samuel

MacFaddon, Captain Thomas
Rocky River church
Magrath, Captain
Martin, Daniel
Martin, Colonel James Nathaniel, North Carolina Militia
Poplar Tent church
Martin, Captain John
Rocky River church
Martin, Captain Nathaniel Marshall
Martin, Captain Samuel, Second North Carolina
Mason, Captain Richard, Second North Carolina
Maxwell, Captain James
Maxwell, James
Maxwell, John
McAnulty, Captain John
Rocky River church
McCall, James, Jr.
McCall, James, Sr.
McCallister, John
McCamon, Charles
McCandlis, John
McCellan, Sergeant James
Rocky River church
McCellan, James, Jr.
Rocky River church
McClenachan, Major Robert
McClure, Ensign James
Steele Creek church
wounded at Hanging Rock August 6, 1780
McClure, Captain Matthew
Mecklenburg Declaration signer
elder, Hopewell church
McClure, Thomas
son of Matthew McClure
Mecklenburg Declaration signer
McClure, Surgeon William, First North Carolina
taken prisoner at Charleston May 12, 1780
exchanged June 14, 1781
McCoy, John
McCracken, John Polk, Jr.
McCurdy, Archibald
Rocky River church
McDow, Thomas
McEachern, Hugh
Rocky River church
McEachern, James
Rocky River church
McEachern, Robert
Rocky River church
McElwee, James
McFalls, Captain John
McGee, Thomas
Rocky River church
McGinnis, Colonel Charles
Rocky River church
McGraw, Benjamin
Rocky River church
McGraw, James
Rocky River church
McGraw, Joseph
Rocky River church
McIntire, William
McKee, Captain Charles
killed at Hanging Rock August 6, 1780
McKillipe, William
McKimene, John

McKnight, Captain Robert
McRee, Captain Griffith John
Steele Creek church
Miller, Captain Francis
Miller, George
Miller, John
Miller, Matthew
Miller, Patrick
Mitchell, John
Steele Creek church
Montgomery, First Sergeant John
Moore, James
Moore, Captain Moses
Hopewell church
Moore, William
Morris, William
Morrison, Alexander
Providence church
Morrison, Duncan
Rocky River church
Morrison, James
Rocky River church
Morrison, John
Rocky River church
Morrison, John
Rocky River church
Morrison, Captain Neill
Mecklenburg Declaration signer
Providence church
Morrison, Robert
Rocky River church
Morrison, William
son of Neill Morrison
wounded and captured at Camden August 16, 1780
mother and sister petitioned and received his release
Morrison, William
Rocky River church

Neal, Captain William, North Carolina Militia
Centre church
Neale, Captain Henry
Steele Creek church
Neel, Captain Thomas
Neely, John
Rocky River church
Nelson, Major John
taken prisoner at Charleston May 12, 1780
exchanged March 1781
Nesbet, Colonel William
Nesbitt, Captain William
Newell, Francis
Rocky River church
Newell, John
Rocky River church
Newell, William
Rocky River church
Ney, Peter Stewart
Nowel, William
Nowol, John

Oliver, Captain
Rocky River church
Orr, James
Osborne, Colonel Alexander, North Carolina Militia
Centre church

Parks, Captain Hugh Jr.
Steele Creek church
Pass, Ensign George
Patrick, Ensign John
Patterson, William
Steele Creek church
Patton, Major Benjamin, Second North Carolina
Poplar Tent church
Patton, Captain Samuel
Petty, Captain Luke
wounded at Hanging Rock August 6, 1780
Pharr, Walter
Rocky River church
Phifer, Colonel Caleb, North Carolina Militia
Phifer, Major John
elder, Rocky River church
Phifer, Captain Martin, North Carolina Light Horse
Pickens, William
Rocky River church
Plunkett, James
Rocky River church
Plunkett, James, Jr.
Rocky River church
Polk, Charles, Jr.
Polk, Captain Charles, Fourth North Carolina
brother of Thomas Polk
Polk, Ezekiel
brother of Thomas Polk
Polk, John, Jr.
Polk, Brigadier General Thomas, North Carolina Militia
Mecklenburg Declaration signer
Polk, Captain Thomas
son of Thomas Polk
Polk, Colonel William, North Carolina Militia
wounded at Germantown October 4, 1777
Porter, Alexander
Rocky River church
Porter, Captain James, North Carolina Militia
killed at King's Mountain October 7, 1780
Porter, Captain Robert, North Carolina Militia
Potts, Captain Jonathan
Powel, Joshua
Powell, Henry
Price, Ensign Reed
Price, William
Purriance, Captain James, North Carolina Militia
Purrians, David
Rocky River church
Purrians, James
Rocky River church
Purser, John

Querry, John
elder, Rocky River church
Querry, William
Query, Alexander
Rocky River church

Rabb, Robert
Ramsey, William
Ray, Captain Thomas
Rea, David
Rocky River church
Rea, Robert
Rea, William
Reed, Captain David
Reed, Captain George, North Carolina Militia
wounded at Ramsour's Mill June 20, 1780
killed at Hanging Rock August 6, 1780
Reed, William
Steele Creek church
Rees, Lieutenant David
Reese, Captain James
Reid, Captain John
Riddey, Thomas
Rigers, Jospeh
Rocky River church
Robinet, John
Robinson, Captain James
Rocky River church
Robinson, John
Robinson, Matthew
Robinson, Robert
Robinson, Robin
Robinson, William
Steele Creek church
Rogers, Hugh
Rogers, James, Jr.
Rogers, Captain John, Jr., Fifth North Carolina
Rogers, William
Ross, Hugh
Rocky River church
Ross, James
Rocky River church
Ross, John
Rocky River church
Ross, Nichols
Ross, William
Rocky River church
Russell, David
Russell, Sergeant James
Rocky River church
Russell, John
Rocky River church
Russell, Robert
Rocky River church
Russell, Robert, Jr.
Rocky River church
Rutherford, Major James

Sammon, William
Scot, Lieutantn Abraham
Scott, Alexander
Rocky River church
Scott, Captain James
Rocky River church
Scott, James
Scott, Ensign John
Rocky River church
Scott, William
Shelby, Evan
Rocky River church
Shelby, Captain Moses, North Carolina Militia
wounded at King's Mountain October 7, 1780
Rocky River church
Shelby, Roce
Shelby, Captain Thomas
Sheppard, William

Shields, William
Shifter, Ensign Charles
Shipley, Edward
Shipley, George
Silver, Nichols
Simmerson, Captain
captured at Charleston May 12, 1780
exchanged June 14, 1781
Simons, John
Rocky River church
Simpson, William
Smith, Henry
Smith, Hugh
Rocky River church
Smith, James
Smith, Ensign John, Ninth North Carolina
Smith, John
Smith, Captain Robert, Fourth North Carolina
Smith, Ensign Samuel, Sr., Second North Carolina
Smith, Samuel, Jr.
Smith, Thomas
Smith, Captain William
Smith, William
Providence church
Snell, Francis
Rocky River church
Spaford, Amos
Spears, William
Rocky River church
Springs, Captain Richard
Stafford, George
Rocky River church
Stafford, James
Rocky River church
Stafford, James, Jr.
Rocky River church
Stafford, John
Rocky River church
Stansill, John
Steel, Captain
Sterns, Captain John
Stillwill, Richard
Stuart, John

Tagent, James
Rocky River church
Taylor, Abraham
Steele Creek church
Taylor, David
Rocky River church
Taylor, Lieutenant John, Eighth North Carolina
Taylor, John
Rocky River church
Taylor, Lieutenant Colonel William
Thomas, Captain John, Ninth North Carolina
Thomason, George
Thompson, Captain James
Thompson, John
Hopewell church
Thompson, Samuel
Townsend, William
Rocky River church

Vance, Captain David, North Carolina Militia
Hopewell church
Vance, David
Steele Creek church
Voyles, William
Rocky River church

Waddington, William
Rocky River church
Walker, Andrew
Walker, Lieutenant Colonel John, First North Carolina
aide-de-camp to General George Washington
Walker, John
Walker, Ensign Nathaniel
Walker, Lieutenant William, Second North Carolina
taken prisoner at Charleston May 12, 1780
exchanged June 14, 1781
Walker, William
Wallace, Aaron
Rocky River church
Wallace, Lieutenant James, Tenth North Carolina
Wallis, James
Providence church
Watson, First Lieutenant Thomas, Seventh North Carolina
Rocky River church
Wauchope, Captain James
Welch, Joseph
Rocky River church
Welsh, Lieutenant Thomas
White, Andrew
Rocky River church
White, Archibald
Rocky River church
White, Archibald, Jr.
Rocky River church
White, David, Fourth North Carolina
Rocky River church
White, Major James
Mecklenburg Black Boys
Rocky River church
White, Captain James, North Carolina Militia
Rocky River church
White, James
Sugaw Creek church
White, John
Mecklenburg Black Boys
Rocky River church
White, Captain Joseph, North Carolina Militia
Rocky River church
White, Samuel
Rocky River church
White, Captain Thomas, Sixth North Carolina
Rocky River church
White, Ensign William, Sr.
Mecklenburg Black Boys
Rocky River church

Whites, William
Mecklenburg Black Boys
Rocky River church
Wiley, Captain James
Rocky River church
Wiley, James
Rocky River church
Wiley, Captain Oliver
Rocky River church
Wilfong, John, Sr.
Williams, Captain Daniel, North Carolina Militia
Williams, David
Steele Creek church
Williams, Captain James L., Fourth North Carolina
Wilson, Captain David
Steele Creek church
Rocky River church
Wilson, Captain James, Tenth North Carolina
Steele Creek church
Wilson, John
Steele Creek church
Wilson, Major Robert
Hopewell church
Wilson, Surgeon Robert, Sixth North Carolina
Hopewell church
Wilson, Ensign Samuel, Jr.
Hopewell church
Wilson, Captain Zaccheus, Sr.
Mecklenburg Declaration signer
elder, Steele Creek church
Wylie, John
Wylie, William
Sugaw Creek church
Wynchaster, Wilson

BIBLIOGRAPHY

Alexander, J.B. *The History of Mecklenburg County From 1740 to 1900*. Charlotte, NC: Observer Printing House, 1902.

Ancestory.com. "Craighead Online." http://freepages.genealogy.rootsweb.ancestry.com/-craighead/articles/name.html (accessed November 8, 2012).

Anderson, William Lee, III. "How Did Mecklenburg County Residents Experience the American Revolution." EleHistory Research. http://www.elehistory.com/amer/mecklenburgDuringAmericanRevolution.pdf (accessed July 10, 2012).

Bethune, Laurence E. "Scots to Colonial North Carolina Before 1775." M.U.S.I.C.s Project. http://www.dalhousielodge.org/Thesis/scotstonc.htm (accessed July 12, 2012).

Blower, David Frederick. *The Orange County and Mecklenburg County Instructions: The Development of Political Individualism in Backcountry North Carolina, 1740–1776, Vols. I & II*. Ann Arbor: University of Michigan, 1984.

Blythe, LeGette, and Charles Raven Brockman. *Hornet's Nest: The Story of Charlotte and Mecklenburg County*. Charlotte, NC: McNally of Charlotte, 1961.

Bolton, Charles K. *Scotch-Irish Pioneers in Ulster and America*. Baltimore, MD: Genealogical Publishing Company, 1967.

Caldwell, David Andrew. "Rev. David Caldwell (1725–1824): Incarnation of a Cause, a Country, and an Age." *Journal of Backcountry Studies*. www.partnershipsjournal.org/index.php/jbdarticle/view/24 (accessed August 5, 2012).

Compton, Brenda E. McPherson. "The Scots-Irish from Ulster and the Great Philadelphia Wagon Road." ElectronicScotland. http://www.electronicscotland.com/history/america/wagon-road.htm (accessed July 10, 2012).

Craighead, Alexander. *A Discourse Concerning the Covenants Containing the Substance of Two Sermons Preached at Middle-Octarara, January 10 and 17, 1741, 2 Upon Joshua IX.15*. Philadelphia: B. Franklin, 1742.

———. *The Reasons of Mr. Alexander Craighead's Receding from the Present Judications of This Church, Together with Its Constitution: To Which Is Annexed a Preface to the Reader, to Discover the Basis or Foundation on which the Reasons are Built*. Philadelphia: B. Franklin, 1743.

———. *Renewal of the Covenants, National and Solemn League; A Confession of Sins; an Engagement to Duties; and a Testimony; as They Were Carried on at Middle Octarara in Pennsylvania, November 11, 1743*. 2nd ed. Philadelphia: self-published, 1748.

Craighead, James Geddes. *The Craighead Family: A Genealogical Memoir of the Descendants of Rev. Thomas and Margaret Craighead, 1658–1876*. 1st ed. Philadelphia: Sherman and Co. Printing, 1876.

———. *Scotch and Irish Seeds in America Soil, the Early History of the Scotch and Irish Churches, and their Relation to the Presbyterian Church of America*. Philadelphia: Presbyterian Board of Publication, 1878.

Dallimore, Arnold. *George Whitefield: The Life and Times of the Great Evangelist of the 18th Century Revival*. 2 vols. Carlisle, PA: Banner of Truth Trust, 1970.

Davidson, Chalmers G. "The Colonial Scotch-Irish of the Carolina Piedmont." Manuscript of an address delivered in May 1975 in Philadelphia to the Scotch-Irish Society of America. Richburg, SC: Chester Genealogical Society and Chester, SC: Chester County Historical Society, 1979.

Dickson, R.J. *Ulster Emigration to Colonial America, 1718–1775*. London: Routedge and Kegan Paul, 1966.

"Encyclopedia of North Carolina: UNC Press—Regulator Movement." University of North Carolina Press. http://uncpress.unc.edu/nc_encyclopedia/regulator.html (accessed February 3, 2013).

Ferling, John. *Almost A Miracle: The American Victory in the War of Independence*. New York: Oxford University Press, 2007.

Fischer, David Hackett. *Albion's Seed: Four British Folkways in America*. New York: Oxford University Press, 1989.

Fitch, William Edwards, MD. *Some Neglected History of North Carolina: Being on Account of the Revolution of the Regulators and of the Battle of Alamance, the First Battle of the American Revolution*. New York: Neale Publishing Company, 1905.

Foote, Reverend William Henry. *Sketches of North Carolina: Historical and Biological Illustrative of the Principles of a Portion of Her Early Settlers*. New York: Robert Carter, 1846.

Graham, George W., MD. *The Mecklenburg Declaration of Independence, May 20, 1775*. New York: Neale Publishing Company, 1905.

Hanna, Charles R. *The Scotch-Irish or the Scot in North Britain, North Ireland, and North America*. Vol. 1. New York: G.P. Putnam's Son, Knickerbocker Press, 1902. Reprint, Baltimore, MD: Genealogical Publishing Company, 1968.

Henderson, Archibald, MA, PhD. *The Revolution of North Carolina in 1775*. Chapel Hill, NC: self-published, 1916.

Historical Committee of 1976. *The History of Steele Creek Presbyterian Church, Mecklenburg County, Charlotte, North Carolina*. 3rd ed. Charlotte, NC: Craftsman Printing and Publishing House, 1978.

Hunter, C.L. *Sketches of Western North Carolina: Historical and Biographical Illustrating Principally the Revolutionary Period of Mecklenburg, Rowan, Lincoln and Adjoining Counties*. Clearfield, UT: Clearfield Publishers, 1970.

John Locke Foundation. "North Carolina History Project: Battle of Alamance." http://www.northcarolinahistory.org/encyclopedia/533/entry (accessed August 15, 2013).

Letterman Associates. "The Scottish Covenanting Struggle, Alexander Craighead, and the Mecklenburg Declaration." http://www.letterman2.com/craig.html (last modified July 12, 2012).

Lewis, J.D. "The American Revolution in North Carolina." http://www.carolana.com/nc/Revolution/home.html (accessed April 20, 2012).

———. "The American Revolution in South Carolina." http://www.carolana.com/sc/Revolution/home.html (accessed May 5, 2012).

———. *NC Patriots, 1775–1783: Their Own Words*. Vol. 1, *The North Carolina Line*. Little River, SC: eBook by author, 2012.

Lossing, Benson J. *Pictorial Fieldbook of the Revolution*. New York: Harper & Brothers, 1850.

Matthews, Louise Barber. *A History of Providence Presbyterian Church, Mecklenburg Country, North Carolina*. Matthews, NC: Route One, 1967.

McGeachy, Neill Roderick. *A History of the Sugaw Creek Presbyterian Church, Mecklenburg Presbytery, Charlotte, North Carolina*. Rock Hill, SC: Record Printing Co., 1954.

McNitt, Virgil V. *Chain of Error, and the Mecklenburg Declaration of Independence: A New Study of Manuscripts: Their Use, Abuse, and Neglect*. Palmer, MA: Hampden Hills Press, 1960.

Morrill, Dan L. *Historic Charlotte: An Illustrated History of Charlotte and Mecklenburg County*. San Antonio, TX: Historic Publishing Network, 2001.

———. "A History of Charlotte and Mecklenburg County." Charlotte-Mecklenburg Historic Landmarks Commission. http://www.cmhpf/org/index.html (last modified February 9, 2014).

———. *Southern Campaign of the American Revolution*. Mount Pleasant, SC: Nautical & Aviation Pub. Co. of America, 1993.

North Carolina Daughters of the American Revolution. *Roster of Soldiers from North Carolina in the American Revolution*. Durham, NC: NCDAR, 1932. Reprint, Baltimore, MD: Genealogical Publishing Co., Inc., 1988.

Powell, William S., James K. Hunter, and Thomas J. Farnham. *The Regulators in North Carolina: A Documentary History 1759–1776*. Raleigh, NC: State Department of Archives and History, 1971.

Powell, William S. "War of the Regulation—Battle of Alamance." Texas A&M University. http://www.tamu.edu/faculty/ccbn/Hewitt/mckstonerrig3.htm (accessed August 13, 2012).

Public Library of Charlotte & Mecklenburg County. "Celebrating the Mecklenburg Declaration of Independence." http://www.cmstory.org/meckdec/bios.asp (accessed July 21, 2012).

———. "The Charlotte-Mecklenburg Story." http:/www.cmstory.org (accessed July 21, 2012).

———. "The Mecklenburg Declaration." http://www.cmstory.org/history/hornets/declare.htm (last modified January 11, 1999).

Rankin, Hugh F. *The North Carolina Continentals*. Chapel Hill: University of North Carolina Press, 1971.

Ray, Worth S. *The Mecklenburg Signers and Their Neighbors—The Lost Tribes of North Carolina Part III—1790 Census by District*. Baltimore, MD: Genealogical Publishing Co., Inc., 1975.

Rouse, Parke, Jr. *Great Wagon Road: From Philadelphia to the South*. Richmond, VA: Dietz Press, 1992.

Scotch-Irish.net. "The Scotch-Irish in the American War of Independence and the American Civil War: They Started the Revolt and Ended It." http://www.scotchirish.net/RevolutionandCivilWar.php4 (accessed November 16, 2011).

Sommerville, Charles William. *The History of Hopewell Presbyterian Church for 175 Years From the Assigned Date of Its Organization 1762*. Charlotte, NC: Hopewell Presbyterian Church, 1939.

Spence, Thomas Hugh, Jr. *The Presbyterian Congregation on Rocky River*. Concord, NC: Rocky River Presbyterian Church, 1954.

Name Origin Research. "Surname Database: Craighead Last Name Origin." http://www.surnamedb.com/Surname/Craighead (accessed February 11, 2012).

TeachingAmericanHistory.org. "Petition from Regulators of North Carolina/Teaching American History." http://teachingamericanhistory.org/library/document/petition-from-regulators-of-North-Carolina (accessed October 3, 2012).

Thompkins, D.A. *History of Mecklenburg County and the City of Charlotte from 1740 to 1903*. Vol. 1. Charlotte, NC: Observer Printing House, 1903.

Thompson, Ernest Trice. *Presbyterians in the South 1607–1861*. Vol. 1. Richmond, VA: John Knox Press, 1963.

Tripod. "North Carolina Regulator's Petition." http://crhailey.tripod.com/regpetition.html (accessed August 17, 2013).

University of North Carolina. "Petition from Inhabitants of Mecklenburg County Concerning Confiscated Property. Documenting the American South—Colonial and State Records of North Carolina." docsouth.unc.edu/csr/index.htm/document/crs14-0367 (last modified March 24, 2010).

———. "Roster of Adam Alexander's Company of the Mecklenburg Country Militia—Colonial and Sate Records of North Carolina." docsouth.unc/csr/index.htm/document/csr22-0125 (last modified March 25, 2010).

USGenweb Archives. "Mecklenburg County, NC—Military—Troops of Mecklenburg, 1776–1897." http://files.usgwarchives.net/nc/mecklenburg/military/mecklenburg.txt (accessed November 23, 2012).

Ward, Henry M. *The American Revolution: Nationhood Achieved, 1763–1788.* Richmond, VA: University of Richmond, 1995.

Webb, James. *Born Fighting: How the Scots-Irish Shaped America.* New York: Broadway Books, 2004.

Whittenburg, James P. "Sugar Creek, War of." NCPedia. http://ncpedia.org/sugar-creek-war (accessed August 15, 2013).

Wikipedia. "List of Battles between Scotland and England." http://en.wikipedia.org/wiki/List_of_battles_between_Scotland_and_England (last modified January 8, 2014).

INDEX

A

B

C

D

E

F

ABOUT THE AUTHOR

Richard P. Plumer is retired after owning an advertising agency for twenty-five years. He wrote *The Town of Suwanee, Georgia: Early History* about his hometown in 2000. It was published by the Gwinnett Historical Society. He has also self-published books on political ideology and meditation.

Visit us at
www.historypress.net

This title is also available as an e-book